The Man Who Loved Schooners

R.L. BOUDREAU

TILLER
PUBLISHING

Tiller Publishing
605 Talbot St., Box 447
St. Michael's, MD   21663
(410) 745-3750

The cover illustration of Captain Walter Boudreau
is by his daughter, Michelle Karolys.

Cover Design: Heather Bryan
Book Design: Peggy Issenman
Printed and bound in Canada

ISBN 1-888671-27-0

Contents

> *This book is dedicated to the memory of my father,*
> *Captain Walter Boudreau.*

ACKNOWLEDGEMENTS

There are a number of people I wish to thank with regard to writing this book. Jeanne Reseigh, Cindy Bradette, and Bob Youden for their unfailing support and honest critique; my sister Janeen Costello, who was a pillar of support along the way. I must thank Dorothy Blythe of Nimbus for taking a chance on a stranded seafarer with an idea and half a manuscript. Most of all though, I owe my lovely wife Sarah-Jayne the greatest debt of gratitude because without her this book could never have been. Through the long nights and the early morning hours she stood the long watch and kept me on my course. The ruthless editor and relentless purveyor of excellence, she is as much a part of this book as I am.

In writing my father's story, I have tried to hold to the facts, and I believe that in the main, I have succeeded in this. However, the passage of time sometimes clouds the best of memories and I realize that some details might not be remembered by all in the way they are recounted here. I apologize sincerely if I have offended anyone, as that was not my intention.

Introduction

The romance of the sea has always stirred deep emotions in the heart of man. From the dawning of time when we first ventured forth in hollowed-out logs, to the great age of sail, the sting of salt spray on our faces has evoked exuberance, courage, and a yearning to search beyond the horizon. In stories and legends, the mariner was credited with virtues such as strength, bravery, and a will of steel. Tales of wooden ships and iron men against the sea have become part of our seafaring legacy.

Those who go to sea are adventurers. From the small boy who hesitates before rowing his punt from the safety of the cove to the open bay, to the yacht master who momentarily ponders eternity before taking his tiny ship across the vastness of the great Atlantic, all sea-goers must sip from the cups of fear and courage. But when they willingly choose uncertainty over security they become adventurers, and the thrill of that freedom is well worth the price.

This is the story of Captain Walter Boudreau, my father, friend, and mentor. We made many deep sea passages together, the first when I was only a few months old. We often talked together over the years, and much of the subject matter covered in this book stems from those conversations. We would sit on deck and watch the sun set, following a passage between the islands, and after filling his pipe he would begin: "There was a time when…," or "I was once sailing to…" and the stories would unfold. He told me of adventures that took place long before I was born, and, of course, there were many of which I was a part.

My father was a man of the sea, and so, this is a story of the sea. The ocean was his home and it was there that he was happiest. In many ways this is his legacy, left to me for the telling. Although I have put pen to paper, it is my father who speaks in the first person, in his own voice, as I recall it. So, cast off reader, as we open the pages of his logbook. Full and by we steer, bound for the port that lies forever over the horizon.

Nova Scotia

I WAS BORN ON OCTOBER 14TH, 1918 in Amherst, Nova Scotia to Dr. Francis and Gladys Boudreau. They named me Guy Walter, but I was always known as Walter. My father broke the long line of sea captains from which we came. When he was a young lad, he made the voyage from Nova Scotia to Fajardo, Puerto Rico on his father's schooner, and was so damned seasick it put him off going to sea forever.

"I like the sailing and the romance of the sea, but my stomach is just not up to it," he told me once.

In my youth we lived in Moncton, where I attended St. Bernard's Catholic School. The nuns tried to encourage me to believe in things that I could not believe, even at that young age. Miracles, the Garden of Eden, snakes who tried to get you to eat bad apples; it was enough to cloud even the clearest mind.

I was under the misconception that all nuns were called "Blessed Virgins" (they might well have been) and made the mistake of addressing Sister Mercedes as "Blessed Virgin Mercedes" one day. This earned me two swollen ears, as well as a few hours' worth of acts of contrition, Hail Marys, and Our Fathers.

I ran into trouble with Sister Mercedes on a number of occasions, and so I tried to improve my image by agreeing to appear in the school play, *Robin Hood*, one year. My mother and father were there in the front row, beaming proudly. I was playing the role of Friar Tuck, and garmented in my brown monk's robe and false bald head, I met Maid Marion.

"And who are you, kind sir?" she asked.

With great pride I stepped forward, and with a voice designed to impress everyone, I replied, "I am Trier F...."

So, in the third grade, I forfeited forever any thought of an acting career and began thinking of something else.

My father fulfilled the picture of a traditional country doctor of that era. He had a cranky old horse and a sleigh, and an even crankier old Ford car. He would go out on house calls at all hours of the day or night, and in all kinds of weather. It didn't matter if it was snowing, raining, or storming, when the patients in the community needed him, he would go. Often he was paid with buttermilk, cheese, fresh meat, eggs, or the like, instead of cash. We lived frugally in the beginning, but my father did well later on, since apart from the practice he developed in Moncton, he made a small fortune in the stock market.

I suppose I first began to acquire a taste for the sea as a boy in Shediac, where our family spent the summers and kept an elderly thirty-five-foot sloop called the *Montrose*. She was a white-hulled gaff rigger, with a small cuddy cabin and a large cockpit. We kept her moored at the Shediac Yacht Club and my father employed a retired sea captain by the name of Eben Hebb to look after her.

I looked forward to the summers at the Shediac cottage, when I could sail on the *Montrose*. Sometimes, I would sit alone in the cockpit after a day's sailing and dream she was a tall schooner sailing to Barbados or some other faraway place. Later, during one of the holidays, my father put me in command of the *Montrose*. I was in heaven, and that summer I sailed my little ship every day. I thought I was quite the captain.

That was until my run-in with the commodore of the yacht club. Returning one day from a sail with my friends, I dropped the anchor in the normal way, putting a stern line onto the dock. The problem was that my stern line was 150 feet long and when the commodore, Hal Weldon, cruised in later that evening with his new motor boat, he got his propeller tangled in the line. This upset him greatly and in his impatience he throttled the engine with the result that the shaft and propeller of his new boat got bent out of shape, and so did he.

Two days later, a very tall mountie with huge polished boots came to our door and asked for the captain of the *Montrose*. I was put forward as that person and for the first and only time in my life, I was relieved of command. My father had to pay for my mistake and it was a long time before I was able to forget that little episode.

My father had a reputation for being a rather tight-fisted gentleman and he quarrelled regularly with Captain Hebb over the maintenance costs of the sloop. On one occasion, just before the beginning of the summer yachting season, Hebb informed the doctor that we would be needing a new set of sails for the sloop, as the old ones were just too rotten to repair. The cost would be thirty-five dollars, twenty for the main and fifteen for the jib. My poor father nearly had a fit. His left foot used to twitch nervously when he was upset, and now it was jumping around as though there was a fire beneath the sole.

"You are a scoundrel and a rogue, sir," he announced, "and I will not pay that amount."

Poor Captain Hebb ended up sewing them himself and without a word of complaint. Later that summer, however, there was an accident aboard the *Montrose*, which highlighted how important it was to keep a boat well maintained.

We were out for a family sail one Sunday. There was the doctor, my mother Gladys, Aunt Gert, Captain Hebb, and myself. It was a brisk sunny day and the *Montrose* was making a fine time of it, reaching past Shediac Island with her rail down. The ladies held onto their bonnets tightly, while my father steered. Whenever there was a good puff of wind, the sloop heeled way over on her side, my mother would quickly offer up a prayer while bracing her feet and glaring at the helmsman. Captain Hebb and I tended the running backstays and the jib sheets whenever we tacked, and all seemed to be just hunky-dory until towards noon, when the wind began to get gusty.

Suddenly, there was a loud report like a gunshot on the sloop. The crew of the *Montrose* looked up in horror as the whole rig came crashing down. One of the wire stays, which Captain Hebb had so pleaded with my father to have changed, had parted under the strain and the mast broke off at the deck.

"Oh my God, the post broke!" cried Aunt Gert.

"Francis, I will never forgive you for this," my mother admonished her husband.

As Captain Hebb and I cleared the wreckage, the rosaries that Aunt Gert and Gladys always seemed to have handy came out and the "Hail Marys" poured forth. No amount of prayer, however, was going to fix the mast and eventually a small motor boat came out from the yacht club and towed us in.

As a result of this incident, my mother absolutely refused to go near the *Montrose* again and she was put up for sale, being deemed a frivolous, expensive toy, as well as a dangerous one.

The memories of the summers I spent sailing in Shediac became firmly etched in my mind. Occasionally we visited Sydney, where my uncles were schooner captains and we would go aboard their ships. Even as a young fellow I knew the ropes. I would drag my father to various parts of the deck to eagerly demonstrate my knowledge.

"Look here father, this is the topping lift, and see here, this rope is the peak jig."

My uncles recounted stories of voyages to faraway lands and adventures on the high seas. My father never realized the affect those tales were having on my young mind. The years passed and my schooling continued. My parents wanted me to pursue a medical profession and gave me as much encouragement as possible in that direction.

"Dental work, that's the ticket," father would say. "There's a lot of money in teeth, you know, and everybody has them."

My sister Yvonne, brother Bob, and I were well provided for and we were sent to good schools and universities. Yvonne married a successful businessman in Moncton and raised her family there. Bob went to medical school. After a stint in the Korean War as a MASH unit doctor, he began a successful dermatology practice in Florida, where he remains to this day.

My own life, however, took a very different course. In 1939 the world was plunged into the horror of total war. I was twenty-one at the time and while still uncertain about my future, I continued earning my degree at St. Francis Xavier University in Antigonish, Nova Scotia.

I was a strong young man with a problem. The war raged and I had to make some serious decisions. The thoughts that swirled around my head were perhaps romantic and unrealistic, but they just wouldn't go away. There was the Army, the Navy, or even the Air Force, but none of these appealed to me. A few of my friends joined the Navy and proudly sported smart blue uniforms with a little gold braid on the sleeves. But my dreams were of tall spars with square sails reaching up to the stars. Instead of brass buttons on a blue uniform, there were sea boots with woollen hats and visions of yardarms over a blue sea. In truth, there was saltwater in my veins and I thought of the generations of Boudreau sailing shipmasters who had gone to sea from the seaports of Nova Scotia.

I was torn between two roads: I felt a certain degree of guilt because my father wanted a medical career for me. However, in the summer of 1941, I took a job that helped decide my future. I went out on a merchant ship called the *Colony Trader*. My friends thought I was insane using my summer holidays to go to sea during wartime.

DR. FRANCIS WAS A GOOD
WHEELSMAN, BUT HE SUFFERED
FROM THE *MAL DE MER*.

I secured the position through the Shaw Steamship Company in Halifax. They sent me to Windsor to join the vessel as an ordinary seaman. I had my own vision of what this adventure was going to be like. A handsome ship sailing across a royal blue sea, steered by swashbuckling tars shouting "Avast there" and "Stand by to batten down the hatches." Fine, brave seamen all, and then there would be the inevitable storm, which I could recount in the bar. The realities were a bit different. For my first real seagoing experience, I managed to choose a lousy ship.

The *Colony Trader* was a rusty old steamship of about five hundred tons, which on a good day might make seven knots. She was small enough that I thought the Germans would never bother to waste a torpedo on her. Nonetheless, it was possible, I said to myself. I was still naive enough at this point to place a degree of romance and adventure on the possibility of being torpedoed.

German submarines were, in fact, torpedoing ships close in along the shore. The tonnage loss of ships going up and down the East Coast was far higher than in the mid-Atlantic. There was heavy tanker traffic along the American coast with oil from Curacao and Trinidad. I read of the weekly sinkings in the newspapers.

Apparently, you could stand on the shore at night and see the glow from the explosions as they lit up the sky. At that point I never thought of the men suffering and dying in the water.

So, I joined the old *Colony Trader* in Windsor, and after four days of loading we got underway with our holds full of fertilizer, bound for Norfolk, Virginia. The ship stank like you would not believe and immediately dampened my romantic notions of being at sea.

The crew held their breath as they ran past certain sections of the vessel where the stench was especially pungent. We were like a square-rigged sailing ship in one respect, loving it when the wind was astern and blowing the stink away from the bridge.

Unfortunately for the rest of the crew, the captain and the mate both turned out to be drunks. It's a wonder we were able to navigate out of Windsor, let alone all the way to Norfolk. We did make it, but I believe it was largely due to the crew keeping the lights of the shore on our starboard hand as we steered.

When we arrived in Norfolk two weeks later, some of the crew refused to "turn to," classifying them as mutineers during wartime. Some felt the ship was unseaworthy and we were held up for six days because the engineers refused to put steam in the boilers.

"This rust bucket is about ready to sink," they exclaimed.

"No need to worry about the Germans, all we have to do is stop the pumps and she'll go down of her own accord," remarked the chief.

"Unsafe and run down," the cook proclaimed, making sure he got in his two cents' worth.

The skipper and mate finally sobered up when the shipping master came aboard with the police. Being the new boy, I wisely kept my mouth shut, but I was also warned by the "veteran" crew members that if I so much as lifted a finger to help get the ship underway, they would "see to me." Great, I thought to myself, not the kind of thing I expected on my first ship. I was, even then, beginning to show an independent streak and so, with a couple of the other crew, I went to the shipping master and told him that when he got the problems sorted out, we would be ready to carry out our duties.

A day later the crew agreed to return to duty after being threatened with legal action and the *Colony Trader* clunked her way back to Windsor. When we made port, those who had been involved in the "mutiny" were hauled off to a hearing, while the two other young men from Newfoundland and I were absolved.

I went back to St. Francis Xavier for the fall semester and listened to my friends recount their holiday experiences. Most of them obviously had enjoyed their holiday, but when they asked me about mine, I had to admit that I had spent it shovelling fertilizer on the *Colony Trader*.

I graduated with a B.A. in May 1942 and spent three weeks at the Medical University of Tennessee. I made the effort in order to please my father, but it was no use. The call of the sea was too strong to ignore, and so I cast off and laid a course for home and the coast of Nova Scotia. My father took the decision in good form. Perhaps he had known all along that I would follow the sea, and once I stated my case, he gave me his full support.

In December of that year, I travelled to Halifax with my seaman's card and presented myself at the shipping master's office. There were men of many different nationalities waiting at the seaman's pool for their assignments. You were given the option of refusing a particular job if you really didn't like it, but sooner or later you would have to accept one or they would take your merchant seaman's card, and then the Army could have you.

The first job that came up for me was a position on an ancient Greek tug, which I refused. Luckily, the next position was the one I had been waiting for. On the last day of December, I took the bus to Louisbourg. The town was quiet and my boots made a crisp sound in the snow as, with shouldered sea bag, I made my way towards the docks. Seeing her spars, I quickened my pace and as her stern loomed in front of me I saw the faded letters *Angelus*, and below it, Montreal.

The *Angelus*

SHE WAS A TRUE WINDJAMMER and I felt as if I had finally reached the place for which I had for so long yearned. Here at last were the yardarms, the canvas sails, the miles of rope, and the men who would show me their use. Resting my seabag on the dock, I paused briefly by her side, looking up at her.

The *Angelus* was a large square-rigged barkentine of 238 tons, and although the white of her previous colour showed through the drab wartime grey where it was peeling off, she was still impressive. She was massively constructed of oak and pine, with a broad square stern and a good looking clipper bow. Her three masts towered above me, and her wide yardarms with furled canvas hung crosswise on the foremast, so that the lower yard sat right over my head.

I was daunted momentarily by the miles of rope and rigging. How would I ever learn their use? But there were thousands before me who had learned the ropes and fought kicking canvas a hundred feet above a pitching deck, and so would I. She had no engine or mechanical contrivance of any kind and we would rely upon the power of the wind alone. As I stepped aboard, two men met me at the rail.

"Your name Boudreau?" one of them asked me. A short, stocky man with a seaman's face and piercing blue eyes, he wore the grey-green coarsely woven woollen-style cap that was de riguer then.

"Yes," I replied, shaking his hand.

"We've been expecting you," he told me in a friendly tone. "I'm Captain Jensen and this is the mate, Art Holmans."

I turned and shook hands with him. He was a big man with shoulders that told of a lifetime of work at sea.

"You been to sea before, Boudreau?" the mate asked me. He had a friendly face and I liked both men immediately.

"Yes, but only in a steamship," I answered a little self consciously.

"Yod dam," Jensen said chuckling, "they're always sending me the ones with no experience. Anyway, don't worry, Art here will show you how we do it on a real ship."

"Just keep your fingers out of the blocks and your eyes open," Art said grinning.

He walked me forward to a curved hatch on the foredeck which led down to the fo'c'sle, which would be my home during the coming months. It was typical of the era, with tiered wooden bunks to port and starboard, and a mess table amidships. The white paint on the walls and bulkheads was faded and peeling, and the wooden deck was bare and worn from the passage of a hundred pairs of sea boots over a score of years. The place also stank like hell, which apparently was normal. The fo'c'sle was empty and all of the crew were topside. I put my sea bag on a free bunk on the port side and climbed back up the steep ladder and through the fo'c'sle hatch.

As I stood there on the foredeck that cold winter day, I looked up into the maze of rigging, square yards and topmasts. This was all that I had dreamed of, a tall ship and good strong men to sail her. How could I have known what lay ahead?

Walking aft, I met some of the other crew. There were a number of Newfoundlanders aboard: Clarence Mullins, John Hillier, Frank Walsh, and Jack

EVEN AS THE CREW OF THE *ANGELUS* STOOD BUNDLED AGAINST
THE COLD BEFORE DEPARTURE, WE WERE DREAMING OF BARBADOS AND
WARM SUNNY WEATHER. I AM IN THE FOREGROUND AT RIGHT.

McCloud. Captain Jensen was a Norwegian with a good reputation as a sailing shipmaster and the mate was also a sailing ship man. Our cook was a roly-poly man who answered to the name "Frenchy." He hailed from a small village in northern New Brunswick.

The *Angelus* was berthed at the docks in Louisbourg, loading a cargo of lumber for Barbados. We were almost finished when the rescue of the *SC709* occurred.

The *SC709* was a 120-foot U.S. naval vessel bound from Norfolk, Virginia to St. John's, Newfoundland where she was to be based in the capacity of a rescue/submarine patrol vessel. She had depth charges and mounted two 20 mm guns and a compliment of twenty-six men.

Coming up along the Nova Scotia coast, the weather began to deteriorate and the *SC709* was having a very rough time of it. On January 21, the weather worsened until it was blowing a full gale and ice began to form on the vessel's superstructure. If the ice became too heavy, she could capsize.

Eventually, despite the crew's best efforts to chip it off, the weight of the ice put such a list on the *SC709* she became almost impossible to steer. Her commander decided to attempt entry into the port of Louisbourg, where they would at least find shelter. But the stormy weather, combined with her poor manoeuvrability, made this a very dangerous move.

Disaster finally struck when she piled up on the reef outside Louisbourg Harbour, where she stuck fast. The vessel was not in any danger of foundering, but all of her machinery shut down when she took the ground; there was no way to heat the ship or to cook food for those on board. As she lay on her side, the freezing seas repeatedly broke over her and she began to look more like an iceberg than a ship.

We, on the *Angelus*, along with everyone else around Louisbourg, soon learned of the plight of the *SC709* and of the various rescue plans being put into motion. The crew of the U.S. vessel were suffering badly from the cold and pleaded desperately over the radio with the shore station to send help quickly, as they felt they would not last long. They were already weakened from the previous twenty-four hours of bad weather and trapped in their icy coffin out on the reef, there seemed to be little anyone could do to help.

Louisbourg was a small fishing town, and there was no coast guard or rescue facilities of any kind. Few of the lobster fishermen were in commission, as they did not usually fish in the dead of winter.

The message from the stricken *SC709* was relayed to Halifax, and a Royal Canadian Navy deep-sea salvage tug was dispatched. The big tug cracked on speed and made her best time northeast along the coast.

Captain Jensen of the *Angelus* was a man of action and realized that if something was not done soon, the men on the *SC709* would almost certainly perish from the cold right before their eyes. Captain Borgen was another Norwegian and a friend of Jensen's. A shareholder in the *Angelus*, he was aboard supervising the loading of the cargo, but would not sail with us. He was a huge blond-haired bear of a man, who had for the last fifteen years gone to Antarctica with the Norwegian whaling fleet, and a finer seaman you could not find. He was one of those rare individuals who inspired confidence in those around him without effort and we automatically respected him for the man that he was. Captains Borgen and Jensen were real seamen in the traditional sense of the word and they knew about ice and rough weather.

The Navy tug had raced full speed from Halifax and was standing off Louisbourg, but could do nothing. She was too big for us to get close enough to the wreck from seaward and they had no way of getting a small boat across to the stricken vessel. The Louisbourg fishermen managed to get the engines in two of their boats going, but they were hesitant.

Borgen and Jensen acted quickly. They called for some volunteers from our crew and every man stood forward.

"We go to the shore now in the two dories," Borgen told us in his deep booming voice.

Jack McCloud and I agreed that we would row together, and so the *Angelus* launched her dories in the broken harbour ice and we pulled to the shore near the town, where we beached. There were two horse-drawn carts waiting for us and we loaded our craft onto them. Our dories were two of the fine Grand Banks type and very seaworthy, especially in the hands of good oarsmen. We transported the dories over the hill through the graveyard and down onto the shore to leeward and opposite the wreck. We could see her very clearly now at about a three hundred-yard distance, totally covered with ice. A vicious freezing wind blew onshore and I felt unbelievably cold. The beach where we stood was straight downwind from the wreck and there was a good surf running. We dragged the dories to the water's edge and gathered around Captain Borgen.

"What we're going to do, boys, is this," he said pulling on his woollen mitts. "We're going to put two fellas in each dory and we're going to row out there and get them poor fellas off before they dies."

I never doubted for a minute that it could be done; Captain Borgen had said we could do it. Two of the other crew pushed Jack and me off, and placing our oars between the hemp-padded thole pins, we began pulling against the wind and the sea. Our dory's bow lifted to meet each wave as it rolled down towards us, and the sturdy wooden craft would rise almost vertically before lurching over the crest into the next trough.

Although it was brutally hard work pulling against the elements, we found that as long as we kept the bow into the waves, our dory seemed able to handle it. I was a strong lad, as was Jack, but both of us soon began shivering violently as the spray drenched us. The sea kept on coming over the bow in great dollops and after ten minutes I had to stop pulling for a moment to bail. Even that was a problem as the water had a mind to freeze as soon as it settled in the bilge. The dory began to ice up, and soon a thin coating covered our craft, but we pulled on. Above the howl of the wind, I could hear Jack grunt with each stroke of the oars and I redoubled my own efforts. Our woollen mitts were soaked and my hands were soon numb. Each gust of wind brought a hail of freezing spray, stinging our faces like attacking wasps. But youth fosters a remarkable strength and resilience, and even at that moment, I managed to find a little humour in the fact that the icy wind froze our mitts to the oars.

Pulling like hell, we finally came into a paltry lee alongside the wreck. We were a few minutes ahead of the second dory, rowed by Captain Borgen and Frank Walsh. While trying to hold onto the rail of the icy vessel we banged our oars against the hull. We were in a big hurry to get on with the job as the cold was almost unbearable.

The *SC709* resembled a huge block of ice. There was a big surge just in the lee of the vessel and our dory bobbed up and down six feet or more. It seemed like ages, but finally one of the glass windows in the pilot house burst outwards and some heads appeared. They were extremely glad to see us, but they were half

TIME WAS RUNNING OUT FOR THE CREW OF THE ICY *SC709*.

frozen and probably would not have lasted too much longer. We helped two men over the rail, and settling them in the bottom of the dory, we pulled for the shore. The *Angelus* crew made four dory trips taking two men at a time, for a total of eight sailors.

When the Louisbourg fishermen saw it was possible to get alongside the wreck from the lee side, they made a couple of runs with their larger boats, taking off the rest of the crew. All twenty-six crew members of the *SC709* were saved that day and I thought nothing more about it.

A lifetime later, when I had passed my seventy-fifth year, I visited Louisbourg again and the site of this event. There is an anniversary each year celebrating the rescue, but as with many things in life, the passage of time had clouded the facts. It seemed that over the years the events of that day had become twisted around a bit, and blame had been placed where it should not have been and credit taken when it had not been deserved. Because of the events that followed on the *Angelus*, and in memory of my shipmates, those fine Newfoundland seamen, I set the record straight here.

The captain and crew of the Navy tug were branded as cowards. This was not so. The tug was too big to get close enough to do anything, and it was not their fault that they were unable to carry out a rescue. The captain, in the practice of good seamanship, could not have put his own vessel and crew in unreasonable danger.

Over the years the true facts regarding who it was that planned and initiated the first rescue attempt were forgotten. The name *Angelus* faded and few, if any, remembered us at all. It was Captains Borgen and Jensen, those fine Norwegian seamen, who planned the first rescue with the dories and it was we, the crew of the *Angelus*, who rowed out through the surf into the teeth of an icy gale that January day in 1943.

Let those forgotten now be remembered, Amen.

The Gulf Stream

FOLLOWING THE *SC709* RESCUE, we prepared for the voyage south. As I stood there on the deck of the *Angelus*, the deep-sea aromas of tarred marlin and linseed oil, along with that of canvas, manila cordage, and salt fish were strong in my nostrils. Looking aloft, I felt a sense of excitement and destiny as I imagined our sails pulling taut and true against a mariner's sky. Although I was soon to realize my dreams and more, I was impatient for us to be on our way.

The *Angelus* had originally been one of the French fishing fleet that quested for cod off the Grand Banks, Greenland, and Iceland. For many years they had come to North Sydney with crews of French, Portuguese, and Spanish fishermen. It was a hard life. The men who sailed on these ships were a special breed and many were drowned or lost every year when the dories went adrift, or the ships themselves were lost in bad weather.

It was a sad fact of life that the Portuguese seamen in particular were paid so little that when they returned home after a long cod-fishing voyage, they could hardly even afford to buy some of the fish they had caught.

These vessels carried as many as sixty dories to the distant fishing grounds, where they would anchor in order to launch these dories. Our Canadian schooners like the *Bluenose*, for instance, were much smaller and carried only a dozen or so dories.

The little seaworthy dories would go far out from the ships in search of cod. Many were lost, however, when the fog came in. The ship would ring its bell calling them back, but often the sound was distorted by the fog and the dorymen would row around for hours trying to find the ship. Many never succeeded.

When the war came, the Allies commandeered many French vessels around the world and the *Angelus* was one. Some Norwegian interests took her over and put

THE BARKENTINE *ANGELUS* INTRODUCED ME TO THE ROMANCE
OF LIFE BEFORE THE MAST.

her into the West Indies trade. Those of us on the *Angelus* felt we would be safer on this type of ship, as the German submarines probably wouldn't bother with an old square rigger. The future would, however, present us with a different reality.

There was never any question of a convoy for us to join. We were too slow by far and would make our way south alone, with the aid of the great trade winds and God's good grace. On March 5, we made an offing for the West Indies. It was a cold, clear morning and the tug towed us out between the heavy pieces of ice floating in the harbour and set us free three miles out. I was before the mast and I was happy. My shipmates were good men and I felt a kinship here that I had not found on the land.

Captain Jensen stood on the poopdeck with his pipe in hand, watching us as we went about our duties. His little black and white dog, Mutty, followed him everywhere. Our skipper knew more about the square rig than most men and I listened carefully whenever he spoke. Our mate, Art, was a good man and I respected him too. Who could have imagined the bitter trials we would face together.

The weather was fine to begin with, although still cold as we began to make sail. There was a favourable wind for the *Angelus*. Being a square rigger, her best point would be with the wind abaft the beam and that is how it was that day. We started by getting the mizzen and three jibs on to get her going with some steerage way and then Art sent Jack and me aloft on the foremast.

"Walt, you and Jack get aloft and loose the gaskets," he said to me, motioning to the windward ratlines on the foremast.

Jack and I soon became friends and we were given the same watch. Each square sail had to be loosened from aloft first and we climbed the ratlines up to each yardarm. Then we went out on the footropes along the yard to remove the gaskets or lines, which were holding the sails in a furled position. We started from the lowest yard and worked our way up. Forecourse first, then lower topsail, upper topsail, t'gallant, and finally royal. When all the gaskets were out, we returned to the deck and began to set the squaresails. Each sail had buntlines, clewlines, sheets, and braces.

"Hold her on south-southeast," Jensen ordered the wheelsman, and the *Angelus* began to move slowly forward.

It was tough work because the running gear was frozen stiff. The ropes were difficult to make fast or coil and my hands soon became numb. However, the sight of the topsail yard arcing slowly across the sky let me momentarily forget my discomfort.

We were making almost due south and the cold northwesterly built to a strong breeze as we gradually cleared the land. We set the mainsail and main staysails then and the mizzen and main topsails. The *Angelus* was a heavy ship and we needed every stitch of canvas to move her along. When we had everything set, Captain Jensen laid a course for Barbados, taking us to the east of Bermuda, and we trimmed everything to suit under the mate's direction. By mid-afternoon, we were rolling our way south at a good eight to nine knots.

All in all it was bloody hard work, but my heart was in it and there was a good feeling on this ship. I was in the mate's watch and spoke to him by the starboard rail.

"How long will we be on passage, Art?" I asked, putting my hand on a shroud to steady myself against the roll.

"Well, give it three weeks and you won't go too far wrong, I think," he replied loading his pipe from his tobacco pouch.

"You been down to Barbados before?" I asked as he turned away from the wind for a moment to light up.

"Oh yes," he answered broadly, "Been going there since I was a seaman in the *Elizabeth Ann Wagnall.*"

"What's it like?" I asked trying to picture the fabled island in my mind's eye.

"Well son, it's a damn sight warmer than it is round here," he said with a chuckle before moving off to check the set of the forecourse.

I laughed and walked forward to the galley house to see what delights Frenchy was preparing for lunch. It turned out to be the standard fare, which would not alter much over the coming weeks. Either salt pork and potatoes, or salt fish and potatoes.

The *Angelus* leaked. It's a funny thing about wooden sailing vessels; they all leak, it's just a question of how much. The hull moves while at sea and the seams open slightly letting the ocean in, which then has to be pumped back out again. It's a vicious circle, the water comes in, you pump it out, and back in it comes again. From the moment we had the ship under canvas, she started to leak and we began to pump.

"Does she always do this?" I asked Jack after our first two hour stint at the big midships hand pump.

"Yeah, you might as well get used to it," he replied. "We'll be pumping from here to Barbados and back."

"But that means we won't ever be able to sleep," I pointed out, a little perplexed. "I mean, if the off-watch crew has to pump all the time."

"Ah, the joys of life under sail," Jack laughed. "That's the way it is, Walt. It's wartime and this is a real economy vessel."

The watches were four hours on, four hours off. Usually an ocean-going vessel might carry three watches so that you have four hours on and eight off, but seamen were in short supply and we only had two watches. A lot of the off-watch time was spent on the pumps, and on first day when the sun set in the west she still had not sucked dry. I thought Frenchy the cook summed it up pretty well.

"Wan fine ship, pomp all day, an still no suck," he said shaking his head. I went to bed with my boots on and almost never took them off. When I eventually extracted my feet after about ten days or so, the stink was so potent it was almost visible. It was a wonder my toes hadn't rotted away. Even during the precious moments when we were able to rest, we were often called from our bunks to go aloft and hand sail. It was brutal work up there on the yardarms in the sleet and the cold, with darkness all around you, but I found that I had an inner strength, which I pitted against the elements.

The weather stayed cold for about six days and then, with the sudden shifting of the barometer, it changed. We left behind the grey-green seas of the north Atlantic and crossed into the deep blue waters of the Gulf Stream. A warm sun shone down onto our ship and the wind came around to the northeast, filling our canvas and giving the *Angelus* a feeling of renewed vitality. We were now in the great trade winds and the days were fine. The war seemed far away from us as the ship rolled ever southwards.

The change in weather brought a warmth to our vessel, which soon began to chase the dampness from the fo'c'sle and we quickly rigged a small line on the starboard side to dry out our wet clothes. The sounds of creaking tackles and the smell of newly warmed tarred marlin and manila filled my nose and ears. Even the pumping seemed less arduous now and I began to look forward to my wheel watches, when I could steer this tall ship southwards through the dark night under a sky replete with stars.

I loved the feel of the warm sun on my face and the friendly blue sky dotted with puffy white clouds gliding over our ship. From time to time, schools of porpoise frolicked under our bow escorting us on our way south. At night, I would go out onto the bowsprit and sit facing aft as the ship sailed towards me. The sound of her bow wave was almost hypnotic and I never tired of listening to its merry swishing tune. I savoured these quiet moments the most and felt this way of life was to be my destiny. During our watches, Jack and I steered and stood lookout and talked about the war and what we would do after it was over.

"I got four brothers and all fishermen," Jack told me. "My father's got a fine schooner and we fish it together. We longline cod on the Banks, you know. After the war I'm going back to Newfoundland to fish. I even got my eyes on a girl up in St. John's. How 'bout you, Walt, what you going to do?" he questioned.

"Well, I'd like to stay at sea, maybe get my papers one day," I replied. The conversation ended as Art came walking aft.

"Alright boys, we got to drop the main topmast staysail, it's getting ready to part a seam," he told us.

As some of the crew set about lowering the sail from the deck, Jack and I went aloft on the ratlines and climbed to the fore topmast crosstrees. With needle and sailmaker's palms, we cobbled the seam before it could open any further. Jack stayed on one side of the sail while I was on the other, and we pushed the big needle back and forth. When we were done, we set the sail again and the *Angelus* sailed on.

Twenty-three days after leaving Louisbourg, Nova Scotia, we dropped anchor in the crystal clear waters of Carlisle Bay, off Bridgetown, Barbados. It was a brilliant day and before long a dilapidated little red tug boat came out and towed us into the careenage, where the stevedores immediately began to unload us.

Barbados was a long awaited reprieve and we made the absolute most of it. We swam in the warm azure waters in front of the Royal Barbados Yacht Club and walked through the hot streets of Bridgetown. The island itself was pretty flat and had the loveliest white sandy beaches I ever had the good fortune to sink my toes into. The climate was perfect too and I took every opportunity to soak up the warm West Indian sunshine. I had found my paradise. The natives were a friendly, happy-go-lucky lot and the stevedores sang catchy calypso songs as they unloaded our ship.

A group of young native boys arrived at the careenage every day to swim and dive for coins. They congregated in the water alongside the ship and shouted up to us, "Shiny one boss, shiny one."

Climbing aloft to the yardarm, we tossed nickels and dimes into the sea where the boys were treading water, and after cleverly retrieving the sinking coins, they would stow them in their mouths and ask for more. I had to stop after a day or so when I realized I had already thrown over a dollar's worth of coins into the sea.

Jack, Frank, and I managed to get shore leave together and we strolled around the narrow streets and explored as much of the island as we could. We passed miles of tall sugar cane undulating in the trade wind breezes and visited plantation houses and sugar factories.

The rum was cheap and as good sailors, we did our duty and drank our full share. But ours was destined to be a short visit, and all too soon the *Angelus* took on a new smell, that of molasses and rum. This was loaded in barrels, first into the hold and then onto the deck.

I learned something then. Superstition was not dead amongst the men who sailed wooden ships. Our Newfoundlanders put up one hell of a fuss when the Barbadian stevedores placed a hatch cover upside down on the deck. This was considered to be an omen of bad luck.

Finally, the *Angelus* was loaded and ready for sea. I did not welcome this moment. We knew it was still cold in the north Atlantic and the warmth of these latitudes was addictive. I did not want to leave.

On May 1, we were towed from the careenage and we made sail just to the west of Bridgetown. Captain Jensen put us on a northerly course and we squared away. I felt a sadness fall over me as I watched the palm trees recede into the distance, but I resolved then that one day I would return to these warm island shores.

War at Sea

As DAWN BROKE ON MAY 19, the *Angelus* was several hundred miles north of Bermuda and approximately four hundred miles off the U.S. coast. The sun rose as usual, but this particular morning brought along with it the horror of war. Sandy, the mate's son, caught sight of something off to leeward and called his father over. Art had a quick look through the binoculars and sent for Captain Jensen immediately.

"Get the skipper right away," he said in voice shaky with fear, "and get all hands on deck."

Captain Jensen came up and it took him only a moment to confirm the bad news. There was a sinister-looking black-hulled submarine on the surface not three hundred yards distant, making its way towards us. Her hull was awash in the swell, but even as we watched, sailors appeared on her forward section around the long barrelled deck gun. A deafening blast shook the air as they suddenly began firing at us; they were so close to us now that they must have been deliberately trying to miss. Three times the German gun thundered and the rounds fell forward of our vessel, lifting great geysers of white water. I was afraid then like I had never been afraid before and I'm sure the others felt the same way.

"Fore braces, let go and haul now," the mate yelled urgently.

We ran forward to the port and starboard pin rails, casting off the lee braces and then we went to the windward side and hauled the yards around taking the wind aback.

"Haul, together now, haul," we chanted.

We pulled desperately to get the squaresails backed. This manoeuvre gradually brought the *Angelus* to a standstill, hove to and drifting very slowly to leeward.

"Get the boat ready to launch, boys, we'll have to get off," Captain Jensen ordered. "And make it quick!"

I noticed him hiding something under his jacket before he went over to the side opposite the submarine. When he felt no one was looking, he slipped the lead-weighted box of code books over the rail, where it sank quickly into the dark depths.

The black-hulled submarine moved in closer and I saw the evil red flag with the white circle and black swastika in its centre. They came to within a hundred yards, and I watched as the German sailors in the conning tower manned their machine guns. They were young boys, and for a bizarre moment it seemed as though they were preparing to take our photograph as they looked down the barrels of their guns. Through the rust streaks on the side of the conning tower, I faintly made out the form of a stylised wolf painted in faded white, and below it the numbers *U415*.

We hooked the tackles fore and aft and launched the lifeboat on the lee side, where the vessel made a bit of calm for us. It was a standard twenty-five-foot lifeboat, lapstrake constructed and painted white. The ten of us, along with Captain Jensen's little dog Mutty, got into it and we rowed away from the *Angelus*. Our skipper had his sextant and chronometer with him, and we managed to grab some blankets and oilskins.

The captain of the submarine signalled for us to come over and we obeyed, rowing to within ten feet of the menacing long black hull. The thoughts of my shipmates must have been the same as mine during those seemingly endless minutes. We had all heard the chilling tales of Allied sailors slaughtered by machine gun fire as they sat helpless in their lifeboats. This was war and the possibility of being shot seemed very real to me at that moment.

We stopped alongside the submarine and lifting the oars we hoisted our hands in the air. I waited for the crack of the machine guns that would rip us apart and I looked into the blue eyes of the young sailor who was aiming his gun at my head. There was no sign of any humanity there, just a coldness that made me shiver and tied my guts into a knot. The German submarine commander spoke now in heavily accented English. He was young and wore the creased white-peaked naval cap of the German Navy.

"Who is the captain?" he shouted down to us, lifting his chin in question.

Captain Jensen stood up in the stern of the boat. Despite his short stature and unimpressive looks, he was a brave man and I admired him.

"I am the captain," he shouted up towards the conning tower. It was difficult because the submarine's diesels were making a racket.

"I am going to sink your ship. Where are you coming from?" the German captain asked.

"We're out of Barbados, bound for Nova Scotia," Jensen replied, cupping his hands.

"I cannot take you aboard, we have no room, so I am going to let you go in your boat."

He then gave us our exact position in latitude and longitude and how many miles we were off the U.S. coast.

"What do you have in your ship for food?" he then asked. "You have fruit, perhaps bananas?"

"We have only rum and molasses," Jensen explained, while opening his palms in a gesture of helplessness.

The German captain shook his head. He did not want to have a barrel of strong rum in his submarine, I suppose with good reason.

"I am giving you twenty minutes to go back to your ship. If you want to get anything, go quickly," he said pointing towards the drifting *Angelus*, and then he waved us off.

Jack and I, along with two others who had the oars, put them in the oarlocks and we pulled away from the submarine in the direction of the barkentine. There were only four oars so we didn't make very good speed. Our vessel had drifted a considerable distance to leeward during the time we were alongside the submarine, and after fifteen minutes it became clear that we wouldn't have enough time to get onto the ship and off before they opened fire.

"Ease off the rowing boys, it's no good," Captain Jensen told us in a resigned voice, "The twenty minutes will be up in a few minutes more."

So we drifted for a few moments, watching the submarine. After exactly twenty minutes the Germans opened fire on the *Angelus*. The fact that the first shell hit the crap house on the stern took me as a bit of macabre humour. It flew up into the air amidst a cloud of smoke and splinters. We were quite close by and the report of the cannon and the screech of the shells as they went overhead was deafening. It was a sound I would never forget.

The *Angelus* stood with her t'gallant and fore topsail against the sky, like something from another time and place, with the Red Duster flying at the peak of the mizzen gaff. She was destroyed very quickly. Shells took her in the belly at water level and I saw her shudder. Flames appeared on deck, flickering up to the sails. Another shell took away her foremast and the spars fell topsy-turvy into the sea. Fragments of planking flew upwards as two more rounds took her in the bulwarks and fire flared briefly near the galley house. Then as abruptly as it began, the firing ceased.

She went down by the bow first, and her stem slid slowly under. She didn't go down all that fast, just very gently, and right side up. Our last sight of her was the flash of red as the ensign dipped below the surface of the Atlantic. The submarine moved off a short distance and it too slid beneath the water, leaving us alone on a vast grey sea.

"Walt, Jack, get the oars out and let's row over there for a minute," Captain Jensen pointed to the pieces of wreckage and splintered wood floating around from the *Angelus* and we pulled off in that direction. "See if we can find anything useful," he told us.

We picked up a couple of two by fours and laid them on board, but there was little else worth salvaging. We then took stock of our situation, every one of us realizing that it was not a good one.

We were somewhere north of Bermuda and south-southeast of George's Bank. The lifeboat was poorly equipped. There were only the four bent oars, and in any case there was no hope of rowing the hundreds of miles to the shore. There were a few tins of milk and some canned provisions, enough to sustain two or three men for a few days, but they would not keep the ten of us for very long. Frenchy opened some tins of Spam and shared it amongst us.

Captain Jensen was holding little Mutty in his lap and he gave the dog some of his share. The frightened little pooch chewed it up gently and swallowed, blinking a few times in satisfaction. We had an old sail and mast and the tiller was serviceable. There was no compass, but Captain Jensen said he could keep us headed west by keeping the pole star on our right hand side. Somewhere over the horizon in that direction was the United States and hope. To the east, lay the vast empty reaches of the north Atlantic and hopelessness.

So we stepped the mast and rigged the sail. It was a gunter rig with slanted yard arm and loose footed sail. It sheeted aft to the stern thwart. The tiller fitted on fine and we lashed it on with a lanyard.

"Steer west," Captain Jensen told us and we tried to keep her on a course that took us in that general direction.

The sun set in the west, so we kept it behind us in the morning and ahead of us in the afternoon. We stayed low in the boat to keep the centre of gravity down and she behaved well enough at first. We stowed our gear and Frenchy the cook sorted out our meagre provisions.

I don't think any of us were under any illusion about our predicament. We were at the mercy of the great ocean. Her alluring call had brought me to this place with the innocence of the landsman, but now the sea was grey and unfeeling. Far from land with no radio, no one would know of our plight. We would need every ounce of luck and skill to escape this deadly crisis. I was afraid, but strangely enough I had no thoughts of death. We had survived the submarine and I felt sure we would be picked up.

The first night and the following day in the lifeboat were surreal to me. It seemed hard to believe that this was really happening, but the bone chilling wind quickly reminded me it wasn't a dream. The weather was cold and the sun never showed itself from behind an overcast sky. At the end of the second day we began to experience some swells.

When there is a storm at sea, it creates large swells, which can occur far from its actual location. At first, there were only the small swells, which swept under the lifeboat and rolled away. The small size of our boat, however, made them appear mountainous.

The storm came on the morning of the fourth day. The big rolling swells began to break and the surface of the sea took on a malevolent mien. There were squalls of gusty wind with snow flurries. Captain Jensen sat in the stern and steered with his little dog in his lap. He was incredibly tired, but kept on steering. His head would drop once in a while and I think he fell asleep a few times, but he would awake with a jolt a moment later and put the boat back on course.

The wind blew stronger, and suddenly the sail blew out. Unshipping the spar, we fought to get the remnant down. Later in the day we rigged the sea anchor, setting it out from the bow. This helped to keep the head of the boat to the wind. The seas broke in huge foamy crests, and we all knew that sooner or later they would begin to break over the boat. We tried to lash down everything, but there was little we could do. The wind was soon picking the tops off the waves, blowing the freezing spray down upon us with a vengeance. We were wet, cold, and very afraid. The storm continued all through the day and into the night.

Captain Jensen didn't want to give up the tiller. Eventually, I went over to him and told him that I would steer for a while and he gave me his seat. There was not much to do except hold the handle and try to turn the bow to the breaking seas as they came, but it did little good. Frank took over the tiller when I began to suffer cramps in my belly and went to lie in the bottom of the boat.

In the darkness of the night, the roar of the breaking waves was terrifying. Inevitably, the moment we had all been dreading arrived. A huge towering sea rose to windward of the lifeboat. I saw the ghostly white foaming crest above us, and as our bow lifted the huge breaking wave took us. The boat rose vertically before falling upside down into the sea and all hands were catapulted into the dark icy water. Opening my eyes, I tried to see which way was up, but there was only a terrible darkness. As I struggled desperately for air, I thought for a minute that this was the end, I was going to drown, but suddenly my head broke the surface. Hearing faint shouts, I looked around to find my crew mates and spotted the grey form of the upturned boat.

Although we had been cold and miserable in the boat, nothing could have prepared me for the shock of the icy ocean. I knew I could not last long in the water and I swam as fast as my tired body would allow. When I finally reached the boat I found myself alone.

"Anybody there?" I tried to shout above the howling wind and raging sea. "Call your name if you can hear."

There were some scattered replies then and I saw the shadowy forms of others close to me, but from Captain Jensen there would be no call. Our brave captain and his little dog were gone.

The Lonely Atlantic

IN THE DARKNESS I COULDN'T TELL who was who, but we climbed onto the bottom of the boat and clung to the keel. The four steel flotation tanks under the seats were keeping her afloat, and when another wave came along we all pushed together and she rolled upright again. We gratefully climbed back in, but throughout the night huge breaking seas rolled her over again and again. I lost count of how many times we went over that night, five or six, maybe more, but each time we managed to right her again and climb back in.

We sat on the thwarts of the boat through the darkness of the night, waist deep in the icy water. I became so numb, it was difficult to keep going. We sang and shouted at the tops of our voices. We even tried to hold hands, but we needed them to hold ourselves in the boat. It gave me some comfort knowing there were others with me, even though I could not see them clearly.

After the first couple of times capsizing, I noticed our numbers were dwindling, but I was far too cold and exhausted to find out who was missing. Frank injured his arm and was getting very weak, the arm possibly had been broken during one of the capsizes.

"God, my arm hurts," he kept saying, but after awhile he went silent.

Art and I tried to hold onto him, but after a time it was obvious he was dead and we let him go. He lay for a moment in the swamped boat and then a wave came and washed him away, and he too was gone.

A cold, gloomy morning dawned and we counted seven of us left in the boat. Art Holmans, his son Sandy, Frenchy the cook, Jack, Clarence, John, and myself. Everything was gone; the mast, the sails, and the oars. We thought we spotted the mast on the crest of a wave some distance to windward, but we had no means of getting to it and anyway, we were too weak to try.

The wind slowly eased and the swells died down somewhat, but the water seemed to get colder. We must have been somewhere just east of George's Bank by then, but we had no means of knowing.

The day after the storm finally abated, Clarence Mullins and John Hillier died, slipping away within minutes of each other. They just seemed to fall asleep. They didn't show any signs of suffering, they were just taken gently. We slid their bodies into the sea, saying a prayer as we did.

Jack was next. He looked over at me for a long while as though wanting to say something, but nothing came. I was greatly saddened as we sent his lifeless body into the sea. As he sank down, Jack's eyes were open and he seemed to look at me. I remembered the laughs and the good times in Barbados. For a crazy moment I thought he was still alive and I stretched down into the water to bring him back, but I realized my mind was playing tricks on me and when I looked again, he was gone.

During the day we prayed and begged for salvation. I prayed hard. I promised God that if we were saved, I would become a priest or bishop, or whatever he wanted me to become, if he would just save us.

As the sea calmed further, I thought we should bail out the lifeboat. I looked around for something to use, finally spotting a small copper tank. I sawed it in half with my seaman's knife; it took me an age to manage that, but I eventually succeeded. We then began slowly bailing out the lifeboat, which was floating with eight inches of freeboard. Sandy took a turn, then I went again, then Frenchy and Art had a go. After what seemed like forever, we had her dry and were finally able to crouch down below the gunwales and escape from the wind and conserve what little body heat we had left.

Sandy died the next day while Art held him closely in his arms. He was trying to keep his son warm, but it was too late and Sandy slipped away. Art wouldn't let him go and kept holding him as tightly as he could. Finally, Frenchy and I went over to him.

"Art, you have to let Sandy go now," Frenchy whispered, gently shaking his arm.

Art cried then, bitter wails of anguish. It was heartbreaking to hear. We took Sandy from him, letting him over the side and he joined the others who had gone into the deep.

We managed to half dry some of our clothes, along with one of the blankets we found lodged under a seat. This helped keep us warm enough to survive. The days and nights merged into a long, endless misery. We had no water and Art and I licked the gunwales of the boat to get a little dew. Frenchy wouldn't do it; he said the boat was too dirty.

The lifeboat was equipped with a miserly amount of emergency rations and we found a few tins of corned beef stowed in the metal locker under the seat. It had stayed closed during the storm, but as I checked each locker, I sadly noticed that there was no water. We tried some of the corned beef, but its saltiness made us even more thirsty and we had to stop eating it. There was a nice tube of toothpaste, though, and we ate that. No one can ever imagine the luxury of eating that white paste. No caviar or cake ever tasted so good.

There were some flares, but because we couldn't eat or drink them they seemed unimportant at the time. One day, we found a plank floating by, covered in barnacles, so we chewed and sucked them, spitting out the shell. They had a little moisture and tasted pretty good. I craved water, but there was none. In desperation one day, I cupped a handful of ocean and tried drinking the salt water, but I threw it straight back up.

"Don't do that, Walt," Art said is a raspy voice. "It'll kill you."

The next day Frenchy went mad. He began screaming and taking off his clothes, saying he was going to have a warm bath. Before Art or I could grab him, he threw all the remaining tins of food overboard and then jumped over the rail himself. His red flannel underwear floated slowly away and we never saw him again.

Everything became a blur of agony after that. We lost count of the days and nights and they became one. There was only the Godforsaken sea, the cold, and the pain. During the day, I sat in the stern with Art taking the bow, and at night we huddled together under the blanket, trying to keep warm.

One day, a shark circled around us for a long time. It was not that big, but it came very close, its dorsal fin slowly slicing through the water. I thought to myself that we must be somewhere on George's Bank. I don't know why I thought that particularly, but I did. There were many fish about, but we had no way of catching them. Once or twice, schools of herring jumped near the lifeboat, some flying right over us, but none fell in. We even spotted a whale close to us one night. I heard it blowing and it sounded like waves breaking on a sandy shore, but when morning came, there was only the lonely ocean again.

I watched a gull or petrel fly alongside so close I could have hit it with an oar. The bird rode the wind on the face of the waves and he ran up and down with his webbed feet. To me, the complacent look in his eye seemed to be an insult. He was free to fly where he wished, while we were prisoners.

We started to go blind. Towards the end, I could only see Art as a blur and shortly after that, we both began hallucinating. One night I woke in a delirious daze, certain I could see the ferris wheel in Paragon Park.

"Art," I croaked, "I know where we are. We're in Paragon Park, see look over there."

As a boy I had an uncle in the park and I worked there one summer. "Here Art, have a hot dog. You want ketchup on yours? Look at the pretty lights, Art."

But the morning brought only the blur of a cold and cruel sea.

Salvation

AT NOON WE HEARD AN UNMISTAKABLE SOUND. Even my numbed brain recognized the distant drone of aircraft engines.

"Art, it's a plane! Quick, get the flares!" I croaked, going to him and shaking his shoulder.

We scampered to the locker under the seat for the four emergency flares, which had survived the capsizings. My hands were cold and stiff, like old seized claws, and almost useless. I had great difficulty holding the cylinder, as I tried to scratch the top off in order to fire it. The flares had all been submerged, but they were coated in wax and supposedly waterproof. A flat three-inch-long match board had to be peeled off and rasped across the top.

We heard the plane again, the sound of its engines closer this time, but the flares wouldn't light, they just sputtered and went out. I was whimpering and tears of frustration came to my eyes as I stood in the boat. Sitting on the thwart, Art held me around the legs, trying to steady me as I struggled to stop myself from shaking.

The aircraft was close, but I couldn't see it. Our vision had deteriorated so much that the sky was only a blur, but I strained and squinted in the direction of the engines. I wanted to see the plane so much, but my eyes were swollen almost shut.

"Please God, let the plane see us, please," I prayed.

I scratched and scratched the match triggers and finally the last one gave a splutter, but it wasn't enough. The flare died after only a second or two and I threw it angrily into the sea. The plane droned away and soon the sound of its engines faded altogether.

I heard a strange sound then, a soft pitiful sobbing. I looked at Art, but he was laying there silent and motionless in the bottom of the boat. It took me a moment more to realize that the sounds were coming from my own throat.

So this was how it would end. For the first time since the sinking, I felt a sense of total hopelessness. All the days and nights of misery were to be for nought. I lay down alongside Art and took him in my arms. He was cold then, so very cold and I couldn't tell if he was even alive any more.

Finally, the tears came. It was surprising that I had enough moisture left in my body for tears, but they fell down my face in great torrents as I cried out in frustration. This couldn't be happening to me, this wasn't how it was supposed to end. I looked in surprise at my left fist, it was bleeding profusely where I had been hitting the wooden frames of the lifeboat, but I felt no pain. After awhile, I pulled the wet blanket up over us and I fell into a deep sleep with Art in my arms.

Then it came again, right overhead. I tried to open my eyes and I saw it, a huge dark blur roaring right over our heads and as it made another pass the wings dipped as if telling us to hold on, help was coming. There was no doubt that they had seen us this time. The aircraft roared overhead again and then it circled us for a while at very low altitude before moving off.

Art and I stood shakily, shouting and waving our arms, just to make sure they had seen us.

"Help, help, yay, yay, yay."

They couldn't hear us, but we shouted at the tops of our lungs until the sounds of the engines faded for the second time into nothingness.

We were saved. I knew it this time: someone would come. Art came to me as the sun set to the west and we huddled together trying to stay warm under the damp blanket.

"Walt, I'm too cold tonight. I won't see the morning." He was moaning and shaking violently.

"You've got to hold on, Art, someone's going to come tomorrow."

I held Art in my arms under the damp blanket through the night and when he shook, I squeezed him until he stopped.

And so, dawn came and we went to our ends of the boat again. Art was very weak now, as well I must have been, and we sat and waited. This was the morning of our tenth day adrift in the north Atlantic.

Then there were voices and the blurry vision of a grey ship's side and netting near us. A destroyer escort had found us; at last we were saved. We struggled slowly up the net, which they hung over the side for us and the tears flowed freely from our eyes. I was grateful, as was Art, but for him it was a bitter salvation. I believe he left part of his soul somewhere to the southeast of George's Bank with his son Sandy.

They carried us below and gave us warm clothes and cigarettes. The cook placed a huge plate of bacon and eggs in front of me, but before I could dive in, the doctor snatched it away. Instead, he gave me a tiny portion of porridge to start with and then more food little by little as time went on. They gave us dry clothes and dry bunks to sleep in with warm dry blankets. I could not find words to convey the feelings we experienced then, save to repeat "thank you, thank you" many times over. One might only imagine how exalted we felt.

The captain called us to his cabin and we recounted our story to him, after which he took the warship in search of the submarine, but it had long since gone. The ship docked some days later in Portland, Maine and we were finally able to put our feet down upon the land again.

Over the years, I have wondered why I survived this ordeal while the others died. Some of my shipmates were bigger and stronger than me. I think that through it all I never accepted the possibility of dying and so I did not. People have said that I have a stubborn streak, and maybe that had something to do with it.

The *City of New York*

AFTER THE *ANGELUS* TRAGEDY, I returned home to recuperate and spend time with my family. My parents were sympathetic about my ordeal, but I was hardened mentally by it and yearned to be once more before the mast. So, after weeks of lounging around, I travelled once again to Louisbourg to take a position on a vessel under the command of Captain Louis Kennedy.

I found the ship at the same docks where the *Angelus* had been berthed a short time before. It was a strange feeling, *deja vu* perhaps? So much that had happened to me had begun at this very place. I walked down the same dock and stood in the same spot looking at the white-hulled three-masted schooner. The name *City of New York* was emblazoned across her broad stern, and her crew was busy loading rough milled lumber and barrel staves for Barbados, along with a few tons of nails in barrels.

She was a massive vessel, with a hull built to withstand the ice. The famous polar explorer Admiral Bird had sailed her to the Antarctic in 1928-29. Her hull from outside planking to the inside panelling was more than three-feet thick. She was destined to be the last of the sail-powered ships on the eastern seaboard still in the cargo trade. Many other vessels had long since fitted engines or surrendered, but the *City of New York* and Captain Kennedy sailed on, holdovers of a bygone era. She was similar to the *Angelus* in that she had no electric: the only power to work the ship came from the arms of the crew and the small diesel donkey engine on the foredeck, which was used to hoist sail and work the ship, as well as load and unload cargo.

A tall, heavy-set man with curly black hair met me at the rail and it took me only a second to figure out who it was. Captain Kennedy ushered me unceremoniously aboard, pointing towards the foredeck.

"Put yer gear for'ard and then you can turn to," he ordered me in a gruff voice.

I threw my seabag down the fo'c'sle hatch and going to the main hatch, joined the other crew. Working on this type of ship was a hard grind and our skipper would prove to be a tough man, but he was one of the old time traditional sailing ship masters, and a finer seaman you would not find.

There was a funny incident a day later involving a young fellow who joined the ship as an ordinary seaman. He had little sea experience, but had a lot to say and chose to offer some advice to our skipper regarding the number of crew we had on board (we were only nine). He walked up to Captain Kennedy, who was working near the rail.

"Skipper, don't you think that we should get a few more hands before we leave? I mean this here is a real big boat you know," the young fellow pointed out seriously, his hands on his hips.

Captain Lou Kennedy was a big powerful man with arms like picnic hams. He turned to the young fellow in disbelief and, quick as a cat, took a swipe at his ear.

"You lazy little sonofabitch," he growled. "This is a fore and aft rigged vessel in case you hadn't noticed."

It was generally accepted that a fore and aft rigged vessel could be sailed with less crew than a square rigger, and we laughed as the young man ducked out of the way. If he didn't have enough sense to keep his mouth shut, he was at least nimble, but he made his way ashore that night and we never saw him again.

There would be the usual wartime economy double watch system on the *City of New York*; the skipper's and the mate's, three seamen to a watch. Winston, our Bahamian cook, would not stand watch. He hailed from Great Inagua and had been aboard for some time. In the coming weeks, he would try his best, but it was difficult to produce anything decent with the provisions he had to work with. He used a lot of lard with every recipe and it all tasted of salt fish, no matter what he was cooking. The rest of the crew consisted of two Nova Scotians from Liverpool and the LaHave River and three more Bahamians from Great Inagua. Captain Kennedy often stopped in either Turks and Caicos or Great Inagua for salt to carry north, and they had signed on there.

We finished loading towards the end of July and on a clear dawn a few days later we secured a tow from the harbour tug. We began to make sail while still under tow, as the tug had our head to the light easterly wind.

Clearing the harbour, our bow began to gently lift and fall as she met the first of the long Atlantic swells. The light sea breeze held the promise of a good sailing breeze later on, and the salty smell of the ocean was sweet in my nostrils.

The halyards from all four lower sails ran through snatch blocks at the base of each mast up to the engine, which had two large drums, one to port and the other to starboard. Sail was hoisted beginning aft, mizzen, main, and foresail. Throat halyard to starboard and peak to port.

We tried to get the three gaffs up as taut as possible with the donkey engine, so as to avoid any work on the jigs, but after the sails filled and everything stretched a bit, we had to go round to all six purchases or jigs and take them up.

Our mate, a Norwegian by the name of Mr. Skitteson or "Skitty" as we called him, led us in hoisting the head sails, tending the downhauls as the jibs climbed the steel stays. I loved the sound of the galvanized hanks; as they went up the wire they made a whizzing noise. Four of us laid on the halyard until the sail was almost up, then two men tailed on the belaying pin while two or three sweated the halyard tight. When each jib was up, it was the purchases again, getting them taut. There is nothing more irritating to a real sailor than the sight of a sagging sail that has not been brought up properly on the hoist.

Soon after the last jib was set, we cast off the tow and the skipper brought her to starboard, filling everything. All hands then trimmed up and coiled down. With a farewell blast on her horn, the tug headed back towards the mouth of the harbour and we were alone.

I felt only elation that I was once again on the great ocean. Although I did not speak much about my recent ordeal on the *Angelus*, my shipmates knew of it and perhaps wondered why I had chosen to return. Who can say? The Atlantic is a strange and beguiling mistress.

We set the topsails later. Releasing them from aloft as was the custom, each of the three sails was assigned a top man. Mine was the fore topsail and taking to the ratlines, I went aloft. After removing the gaskets from the sail, I shook it out a bit and made sure it was falling out clear to leeward.

"All clear," I shouted down to the deck.

The deck gang hauled away on the halyard, sending the sail up the topmast on its hoops. I made sure that it ran free and the clewlines did not foul. My next job was to send down the tack on the windward side of the gaff. I sat on the jaws and lowered the line. It was easy at first, but the closer it came to the deck the heavier it became, so that by the time I reached the last twenty feet, which was heavy wire cable, it was almost too much for me to hold. The tack cable was full of "meat hooks" and I cut my hands pretty bad lowering it. For the remainder of my time on the *City*, my palms were always cut in some place.

When the tack was clear to the deck, I called down "haul away" and the boys below sweated it down. The last step was to sheet her home, which they finished before I regained the deck. This process was repeated three times as each topsail was set and then finally the big *City*, under full canvas, settled on the port tack with the wind abeam, Barbados bound.

In fact, we were making a voyage which had a long tradition in the history of Nova Scotia. The trade and friendships between the Maritimes and the West Indies went back many generations. The basis of this trade was salt codfish. The schooners that traditionally sailed south on these voyages carried the salt fish, which was a staple in the islands. There would also be nails, barrel staves, and other general cargo. Many of the fast Nova Scotia fishing schooners, when retired from the Grand Banks, ended their days in the island cargo trade, and there were still a few sailing in the West Indies as late as 1969.

The local shipwrights and sea captains of the Caribbean copied the lines of the swift schooners from the north and a thriving shipbuilding trade developed in the islands. The masts for these vessels all came from Canada, as did the timbers for their construction. The local island schooners were slightly smaller and more robust, designed for cargo capacity more than speed. The Nova Scotia schooners returned home with molasses from Barbados and the Windward Islands and salt from the Turks and Caicos. The fine island rum, which Nova Scotian seaman have traditionally been so fond of, came in barrels which were quickly appropriated by the liquor commission and cut down before being sold to the people.

The ship began to leak as soon as we were under canvas and never stopped while we were at sea. Kennedy didn't need to have anyone check the level of water in the vessel because he knew how she leaked. He ordered two of us on the pumps as soon as we were squared away.

We stood our watches and when I was not at the helm I was at the pump handle. It was a test between the vigour of youth and the might of the Atlantic ocean, which seemed more than determined to find its way into the bilges of our ship. At six-foot-one and 195 pounds, I was a stout lad and without boasting, I can say I was strong, but it was still hard-going. The off-watch crew were required to take care of deck work during the day and it seemed as though whenever I put my head down, I was called to the pumps. I learned to hate the "P" word like no other. At one point, when we were five days out, we encountered strong gale conditions for twenty-four hours and the ship began to leak badly. I was called at half-past-one that night, after only an hour in my bunk.

"Hey Boudreau, get yer arse on the pump," Kennedy shouted in my ear. I pumped for two hours by myself until I was exhausted and could do no more. Then it dawned on me. No one was going to relieve me or tell me to stop. I was due back on watch in half an hour. So I left the damned thing, and making my way to the fo'c'sle, collapsed on my bunk.

After two weeks at sea another aspect of life on the *City* dawned on me. Kennedy was wont to clobber his crew for the smallest transgression. More often it was the Bahamians, but the two men from Liverpool got it as well. He seemed to use those big fists of his with alarming frequency and these were not slaps on the head. When Kennedy gave you a blessing with those big paws of his, you were likely to end up laid out on the deck. There was one occasion when he became impatient as I was untying a knot that was seized swollen by the salt water. I could see him thinking about it then, but I looked him square in the eye and he let it pass.

We arrived in Barbados after a eighteen-day passage and anchored in the roadstead of Carlisle Bay. There was no berth available for us and we would have to remain in the anchorage until one became free. But it was a wonderful feeling to be back again and I took a moment to remember the happy days I had spent here with my *Angelus* shipmates.

The Bahamian crew members quickly hauled out their fishing lines and began jigging over the side. They caught a selection of good-sized red snapper and Winston fried them up. Despite his impatience, the skipper enjoyed watching the boys catch fish and was partial to eating them as well. We swam over the side in the afternoons, diving off the ratlines. Our skipper paced the decks, stopping occasionally at the rail to see how the fishing was going. He carried his binoculars, and would put them to his eyes every few moments to see if there was any activity ashore.

Finally, on the morning of the third day, the small red-hulled tugboat came out to pull us into the Bridgetown careenage, where we would unload our cargo. They put a line on the head of the vessel and we heaved up the anchor. The crew of the tug were a different lot from the men who had towed the *Angelus* and there was a lot of screaming and shouting by the Barbadians this time.

"Had ah poat, had ah stahboad, pull de damn line. Wah happen, you wan to mash up de vessel or what?" we heard them shouting from ahead.

The driver of the little tug was either drunk or totally inept. It seemed almost certain they would put us on the rocks near the entrance and Captain Kennedy stood aft by the wheel cursing and muttering under his breath. After weaving around this way and that, they somehow managed to pull the *City of New York* into the careenage, where we were unceremoniously slammed alongside the wharf at the north end. Our skipper had some choice words for the tug boat crew and they were lucky to get paid.

I loved being back in Barbados again, and with what little time the crew had off, we invaded Bridgetown and swam in the warm water off the old Aquatic Club. Being alongside the docks, we only had to stand deck watches and therefore managed to go ashore quite a bit. We caught up on the news and felt lucky after looking at the Atlantic shipping losses in the harbour master's office.

I read a newspaper that was a few days old. It gave a report of the sinking of the *Lady Nelson* and the *Umtata* in Castries Harbour, St. Lucia, an island only ninety miles to the west. A German submarine sailed right into the harbour in broad daylight and torpedoed the two steamships as they sat at the dock. The submarines were still there, like sharks waiting for unsuspecting prey to come along.

While in Barbados, I met an English family called the Toppins, who very kindly took me to their home for dinner one night. They asked me to bring a big Canadian dog for them the next time I came south, as there were for the most part only small mongrel breeds on the islands. I promised to do so.

The stevedores spent two weeks casually unloading our lumber. Kennedy was annoyed about this, as he would have much rather used his own crew, and avoided the stevedore fees, but the harbour master insisted that he use the local men.

Winston purchased a large sow, which he butchered on the foredeck and we had a number of delicious roast pork dinners with fresh island vegetables, which was a real treat.

During working hours we laboured on the ship. There was always some kind of repair and maintenance to be done, typical of large windships. We sewed sails and overhauled the rig as necessary. All too soon, though, our sojourn in paradise was over and Captain Kennedy came to us one afternoon with the news that our holiday was over.

"Time to leave the life of sogering, boys, and get back to being sailormen. We're bound for Great Inagua tomorrow morning bright and early so get your sleep tonight," he told us.

That afternoon the stevedores helped us cover and batten down the hatches and we prepared the vessel for departure.

There was the expected shout just before daylight and we rolled out of our bunks and shuffled to the galley, where Winston had some of that awful black liquid he called coffee ready for us, along with some baccalao cakes.

It was normal and obligatory for a sailing ship of our tonnage to accept the services of the little red tug in leaving the careenage, but our redoubtable skipper was not about to pay this fee if he could avoid it. I was surprised, however, when Captain Kennedy told us we were going to sail the *City* out ourselves. How he would manoeuvre this huge ungainly sailing vessel within the confines of the small basin, I had no idea.

He had us put a doubled stern spring line on the dock bollard and ordered everything else cast off. As the *City's* bow edged away from the quay, Skitty called for the three head sails. The first of the sun's rays lifted above the eastern horizon and a gentle breeze filled the jibs, pulling the ship's head around. I held my breath as our long bowsprit swung slowly down the wind. It looked as though we would rake one of the local trading schooners moored directly across from us, and a number of their crew scampered ashore in fright. The tip of the heavy wooden spar cleared them by only two or three feet, and after it had passed, I breathed again.

When our bow was facing down the narrow channel, Kennedy ordered us to cast off the stern spring line, and casually turning a spoke or two of the helm (as if this were an everyday affair), he sailed his big schooner out to the open sea. Just as we left the confines of the careenage, one of the Barbadians from the harbour master's office came running down the quay.

"Ay man, Come back, nuh. You got to use de tug," he yelled at the departing schooner, but Kennedy just grinned from ear to ear and waved back shouting: "Not bloody likely."

That afternoon found us on the starboard tack under full sail on a course to clear the northern Leeward Islands. She was light this time and the big *City of New York* bobbed around with quite a different motion.

Seventy-two hours later, we cleared the treacherous reefs east of Anegada and the skipper let her off to port. With sheets eased, we laid a northwesterly course to the west of Navidad and Silver Banks towards Great Inagua, where we would load a cargo of salt.

At dusk seven days later, I saw the famed salt mountains for the first time. The island itself was very flat, as were most of the Bahamas, and we saw the salt mountains before the land. They looked oddly like icebergs floating in a tropical sea. The Bahamian shelf comprises a lot of very shallow water and we had to drop the anchor almost a quarter mile offshore.

The Morton Salt Company began to ferry the snow white rock salt out to the anchored schooner at daylight and this time we did all of the loading ourselves. It came out in fifty foot wooden barges, called lighters, pulled by an antiquated motor boat, four at a time. We took two to port and two to starboard and loaded the coarse salt with slings and the donkey engine. The men in the lighters filled the canvas slings with shovels, and with the donkey engine and one of the gaffs, we lifted it aboard and emptied it into the holds. It was a slow process.

We worked from dawn to dusk every day and the level of the salt in the holds gradually began to rise. After a week of loading, Jeffrey, one of the Bahamian crew came forward to ask Captain Kennedy for some "off time." He had not been home for a while and wanted to visit his family. It was mid-morning and the work was in full swing. We watched as he walked to the rail where the skipper was standing. Because of the noise of the donkey engine, we couldn't hear the words that passed between the two, but the results of the short conversation were seen by all. Kennedy chased Jeffrey around the main hatch and when the Bahamian reached the other side he took a flying leap over the side. Everyone stopped working for a moment and moved over to the rail to see if Jeffrey had drowned, but he was a strong swimmer and after a few seconds his head bobbed to the surface and he set off swimming for the shore. I was worried because we had seen a number of big sharks near the anchored schooner, but he made it ashore in surprisingly short order, and that was the last we ever saw of him. I resolved that I would do without shore leave in Inagua.

The last of the salt was finally loaded, and with one less hand, we made sail in the lee of Great Inagua for the voyage north to Nova Scotia. Passing into the Atlantic ocean just north of Hogsty Reef, we spotted a rusting freighter hulk that had come to grief while trying to clear the land. Captain Kennedy, however, was an excellent navigator and we passed well clear. Once in the deep ocean, it was back to the usual routine; steer and pump, steer and pump.

As the sun rose slowly eighteen days later we found ourselves off the Nova Scotia coast. We were close hauled on the port tack under full sail and making good time, despite our belly full of salt. The wind was forward of the beam at about twenty-five knots and we lay within sixty miles of our destination—Lunenburg.

Unfortunately, our course had caused us to lay more offshore than we would have liked and as a result we would have to tack to make the land. This was a word we didn't like to hear on the *City of New York*. The ship's design had left her well suited for carrying a big cargo, but a fine sailer she was not. The *City* had a deep, wide hull section and she carried her beam well fore and aft, giving her a fine motion at sea and excellent directional stability. However, all these characteristics resulted in a vessel that would not tack very well. Vessels of this type were notorious for coming into "stays" or "irons" as it is called. This nautical predicament occurs when a sailing vessel is caught head to the wind with canvas flogging and unable to fall away and fill on either tack. The *City of New York* was a very reluctant ship when called upon to bring her bow through the wind. Whenever we tried to tack, she would inevitably slew around very slowly and after losing headway, fall slowly back onto her original course, or worse, into irons.

Towards noon, our skipper figured we had made enough to windward to fetch Lunenburg and he would try to tack her soon. This would be the only tack before making port and we made the preparations. We rigged the mizzen boom tackle to port, so that it could be hauled out in order to help bring the schooner's stern to starboard. The foredeck crew would back the head sails to starboard, helping the bow to fall off to port. The topsails would have to be tended as well. The mizzen, which had no triatic stays to hamper it, would tend itself, but the main and fore topsails had to be clewed up every time and dropped on the other side of the stays. The tacks then had to be hauled aloft each time and sent down the windward side of the gaff as well. This operation was no simple task.

When all had been made ready, Captain Kennedy called the mate over.

"Skitty, we're going to tack her first time around, so make sure the boys move fast."

Although doubtful, the mate gave the affirmative and motioned us to our various positions. Mine was aloft on the foremast.

"Stand by to come about," the skipper called, followed a moment later by, "Ready about," and finally "hard-a-lee," as he put the helm over.

In the traditional way, we loudly repeated each order in acknowledgment.

From my perch in the fore topmast crosstrees, I watched the big ship slowly turn to port. Spinning the wheel hard over, Winston and Kennedy hauled the mizzen out on the boom tackle. The rest of the hands attended the jib sheets and the topsail clewlines.

Well, she did not come about. Nor did she come about after a dozen more attempts; she just would not do it. She kept slewing around and after coming close to irons, would fall off on the port tack again. She might have done it, but the short steep sea was stopping her from carrying her momentum through the eye of the wind.

Captain Kennedy was a stubborn man. He cursed and swore, and as night fell and I stayed aloft in the foremast crosstrees we continued to try and tack the schooner. My hands were bleeding freely from the wire tack cables and I was exhausted. I will never forget that night, alone in the darkness, with the heavy gear crashing around every time the ship came into the wind. Finally, after many hours we wore the ship around and made Lunenburg the following morning.

Many, including myself, thought that Captain Louis Kennedy was a bit of a rogue and could be a hard man. But we were living the last of the true days of sail and this way of life demanded tough men. During my years at sea I met many sailormen, but Captain Kennedy was perhaps the finest seaman I ever had the honour of sailing with. I admired his strength and determination and this is borne out by the fact that I named my first born son, Louis, after him.

I made a second trip to the islands with Captain Kennedy and brought a cute little black Labrador puppy to the Toppins. The voyage was a mirror of the first and we met no submarines. I did, however, adhere to an earlier resolution and after the ship was berthed in Liverpool upon our return to Nova Scotia, I signed off articles and went home to see my parents for a few days of well deserved rest.

Captain Lou Kennedy became somewhat of a legend in the West Indian islands and stories of him and his first schooner, *Sea Fox*, were told in the waterfront bars and taverns. The *Sea Fox* had been a 135-foot topsail schooner and fast as hell. She normally would have carried a crew of ten or so, but one year, Kennedy sailed her to the West Indies with only himself and one other crew member aboard. He always thought he was a good as two or three regular men at sea and, in truth, he probably was. He arrived in Barbados that time, only to find himself in trouble with the harbour master, who refused to believe that only two people could have sailed this big schooner down from Nova Scotia.

"Captain, I want to know what happened to the rest of your crew?" he asked, suspecting foul play. But he did not know Lou Kennedy.

In later years I met up with him in various ports, when he was sailing around in his ketch, *Alpha*. We would often share a bottle of rum together and regale each other with stories. Never once did he fail to drink me under the table.

Today, there rests a large painting of the schooner, *Sea Fox*, in the hall of the Royal Barbados Yacht Club in Bridgetown. It is sad to think that most of the people who walk by it every day know nothing of the great seaman who was her master.

Labrador

In early 1945, while in Sydney, Nova Scotia, I bought the *Nellie J. King*. I wanted my own schooner and after a verbal pitch worthy of a politician, my father gave me the required financial help. I had been to the West Indies in big schooners and figured that if I had to face German submarines and bad weather, then I would rather do it while making my own money.

The 115-foot *King* was a former rum-runner and a good example of the fast fishing schooners built in Nova Scotia in the early 1900s. Fore and aft rigged and gaff headed, she had a pretty clipper bow with a long graceful sheerline, ending in a stern that was perhaps a bit more yacht-like than most. Her spars were slightly raked and her main boom and bowsprit stretched out way past her ends, giving her a sleek and speedy look.

I paid three thousand dollars for her and was well pleased with the deal, but the realities were a bit different. Since her rum-running days, when she had made a lot of money for her owners, the *Nellie J. King* had seen some lean times. By the time I got her, she was showing signs of neglect and her long graceful sheer was beginning to hog. In truth she was old and leaky, but the wonder of romantic youth blinded me to any faults she might have had. As far as I was concerned, I owned the *Cutty Sark*.

Some years earlier, she had been fitted with a big two-cylinder engine. This was a questionable asset, as it rarely worked and the propeller took a knot or so off her sailing speed as it dragged uselessly through the water. Even when it did work, it pushed the schooner at only two or three knots, and that was in flat, calm water. If there was any kind of a head wind or sea running, she just stopped dead. The engine itself was a man mauler. It had a huge flywheel, which had to be cranked with a long handle to get it going, and if you weren't careful it could catch you when the engine fired, causing a serious injury.

She also leaked a bit. To be honest she leaked like hell, just sitting in port, let alone when she was at sea. Nevertheless, I thought she was the finest ship ever built and after closing the deal, I spent a few more dollars on her. We gave the topsides a new coat of black paint and replaced some running gear. I bought a set of used sails and had them recut and we re-seamed her deck. I bought two hundred feet of flag halyard line and the final touch was a big Red Duster flying from the main peak.

THE *NELLIE J. KING* WAS OLD AND LEAKY BUT I OWNED HER AND THOUGHT SHE WAS THE BEST.

There was not a prouder man on the waterfront the day we left port on our first voyage, and I strutted around her deck like a king. I was a ship owner now and too bad for the rest. The fact is, I didn't have enough experience to command her legally or otherwise, so I hired a well-seasoned captain by the name of Emmett Cruikshank. Placing myself under his command, I would serve as the vessel's mate. Even though I was the owner, he would take the responsibility for navigation and operation of the ship and I would obey his orders.

Emmett was a stout balding fellow who reminded me of W.C. Fields in more ways than one. He chewed tobacco, and in a holdover from his days as a deck seaman he kept his plug in the crotch of his underwear.

"Ain't nobody going to ask me fer none if I keep her stashed down there," he explained to me. I felt it was sound reasoning.

We had a crew of six deckhands, five of whom were Mi'kmaqs from Cape Breton and a cook from Liverpool, Nova Scotia.

Thus began an idyllic period of my life. We started by shipping general cargo and fresh produce to and from Prince Edward Island. We carried lots of spuds and ate them in large quantities while on passage. Any loss in cargo weight was put down to bad weather.

The *Nellie J. King* spread her patched wings and we sailed her into the Strait of Canso and through St. Peters Canal. Our schooner ghosted across the tranquil waters of the Bras d'Or Lakes and through the narrows. I marvelled at many of the most beautiful bays and coves that God ever created. Once, while anchored in a quiet cove, some fishermen came out to us in a lobster boat. We exchanged some cabbages from Prince Edward Island for two lovely fat salmon, boiling and eating them just an hour out of the water.

There were other schooners in this coastal trade and we got to know them well. We had a sort of brotherhood. Sometimes we found ourselves anchored together in some bay or village, and one of us always seemed to be able to dredge up a hidden bottle of the French Martinique rum, which we shared on the deck, recounting dubious tales of great seamanship and past adventures. The months flew by almost unnoticed, borne by the exuberance of youth and the lure of the sea.

We sailed along Nova Scotia's rugged coast and gradually the entries in my seaman's book increased. I was looking forward to the time when I could sit for my master's ticket and so command my own vessel.

We began carrying general cargo to Newfoundland and St. Pierre and Miquelon. Inevitably, we shipped some extra cargo back from the French islands in the form of cases of rum, undeclared of course. We carried coal as well, from Sydney to Newfoundland. When the holds were full, we often carried a deck load too. We fitted side boards and stacked the powdery coal until it was six feet high. Sometimes, we loaded the old *Nellie J. King* until her decks were almost level with the water.

One of the little tricks I had learned from Captain Kennedy was the "movable" plimsoll mark. This allowed skippers to overload their vessels whenever they thought they could get away with it weather-wise. It was dangerous to go to sea like this, but those extra tons were the extra dollars that kept us going. In the remote northern areas off the Newfoundland coast there was often bad weather, especially in late fall. Then the fine days were just the moments between the storms.

In St. Pierre, I enjoyed the dark rum of the southern islands and discovered the great philosophies that reside in the bottom half of the bottle. Emmett had quite a taste for it as well. That summer, the *Nellie J. King*, with a general cargo that included two dozen head of cattle, made port in St. Pierre. It had been a lousy trip. Those poor cows must have been constipated for weeks, saving it up especially for us. I rigged a gantline fore and aft on both sides amidships and we tied the cattle there. They pooped all the way to St. Pierre. Some got seasick as well. It was the strangest thing, those great bovine beasts would look back at me and "moo" before shaking their heads and then it was "heave ho."

Emmett was impatient to have our cargo unloaded and when all was finally ashore he wasted no time in heading for the bars. He was wont to become quite religious whenever he had a skinful and on this particular occasion he was at his most holy eloquent. At the two waterfront bars in St. Pierre that night, Captain Emmett bestowed blessings upon the local fishermen and seafaring men and I arrived at the first bar just as he began.

At a moment precipitated by something known only to him, Emmett climbed shakily onto a table and stood up, spreading his arms. "God bless you all, God bless you, God bless every one of you." After a dozen or so blessings he dismounted for another drink, whereafter he looked for another suitable table top from which to preach. The locals took it fairly well and apart from one fellow pelting an empty beer bottle at him, there was no real trouble. However, in the morning when we were ready to depart, our captain was nowhere to be found.

"Anyone seen Emmett?" I asked my crew.

"Nope, we ain't seem him nowheres, Walt. He didn't come back aboard last night," they replied just as puzzled as I was.

A couple of the boys and I went ashore and searched everywhere, from the church to the schoolhouse without any luck. Eventually, we found him laid out at the back of the fish warehouse, sleeping with his mouth was wide open and reeking of the sweet Martinique rum. Bending forward to have a look at him, we noticed a small cloud of flies. They rose from his mouth when he exhaled and returned as he breathed in. There were a few rats scurrying around and I wondered how many of them had been into his mouth without his knowing it. Truth be told, we heard him long before we saw him, as in the quiet of the morning his snoring carried way down the street.

"Come on Emmett, we've got to leave now," I shook him and he slowly came to, holding his arm over his eyes.

"What? What, she leaking again? Well, just pump her out and call me when she's dry." Emmett made to roll over again, but we took him by the elbows and walked him down the street.

We finally got underway after another battle with the temperamental engine and laid a course for Sydney. Emmett was having a hard time of it and vowed he would never touch the rum again.

"As God is my witness," he declared looking at me with beet-red eyes, "I'll never touch the stuff again." This was, of course, a short-lived resolution.

At the end of September 1945, we left Sydney and headed north, bound for the Straits of Belle Isle. We had a full cargo for a military site on the Labrador coast. We left with our holds filled with one hundred tons of coal as well as the typical deck load. This wasn't as bad as it sounds, because after two or three days at sea, half of it was often washed overboard. We also carried thirty drums of fuel oil and a few thousand fresh eggs. There were crates and crates of eggs piled high on the deck.

From the start of the voyage the weather was fickle. We were weather-bound in Cornerbrook with a couple of big Newfoundland schooners waiting for an improvement. We spent three days there and the ground was blue with blueberries. I sat in the hills surrounding the harbour and ate them by the peck, admiring my ship anchored below.

At daylight one morning, we followed one of the big Newfoundland schooners out, laying a course for the Straits of Belle Isle. The weather was overcast and ominous looking, but as I felt that I had the *Cutty Sark*, nothing could harm me. However, the weather began deteriorating very quickly, as it would in these parts. Throughout the day, dark low clouds scudded overhead assisted by a stiff southwesterly and the *King* flew northwards. The old wooden vessel seemingly recaptured her youth as, with building winds on her quarter, she sunk her lee rail to reel away the knots under the four lowers. But even then, Emmett began to worry. The stress on her ageing hull was causing her to leak even more.

It grew cold and miserable and we donned our sweaters and oilskins. That night, the weather worsened and by morning there was a nasty sea running. By ten o'clock the wind was gusting of a strength that threatened to blow out some canvas. It was time to shorten down.

"Walt, get the boys and get rid of the main. I'll run her off for the jib when you're ready," Emmett said to me.

We set the storm trysail as soon as we had everything squared away. We kept the foresail and jumbo. The schooner seemed happier under this rig and we continued to claw to windward. I thought it couldn't possibly get any worse, but worse it got until it was howling.

We could see the coast of Labrador now, low and far to leeward. South of our destination and with the wind a bit ahead, the *King* was making heavy going of it and taking a lot of water on the deck. Most of the deck coal was gone by now, washed away by the waves, but the oil drums and the eggs remained.

As the day wore on, the sky darkened and the wind steadied at a good strong gale, but hauled around a bit more to the east. This was bad news for us, as it put us on a lee shore and there was a huge sea running.

By mid afternoon, we knew we were in trouble. It was the traditional seaman's nightmare: A sailing vessel off a rugged lee shore in a gale. Emmett pointed to the headland ahead of us some twelve miles distant.

"That's Cape Diable and I think there's a place just past there called L'Anse au Loup, or "Bay of the Wolf." We should be able to find a bit of lee there to anchor and sit this out," he said spitting some tobacco juice to leeward.

"You sure, Emmett?" I asked cautiously.

"Well, I think so, been there a few years before you know," he replied, not sounding too convincing.

We agreed to give it a try, but we had to get around the headland first. The coastline from our position to the headland was rugged and stark, and even now we could see the huge seas breaking on the rocks to leeward, flying into the air in great sheets of spray.

There was no place for us to get onto the land here, even if the schooner went ashore. Our only hope was to clear the headland. The "bitch," for that was what we called our decrepit old engine, would not give us even a hint of a beat, and after we had cranked until we could crank no more, we gave it up. We were worried that if we tried to tack under this reduced rig she might not come about and would fall off to leeward. Even if we did manage to tack, it would not greatly improve our situation because the wind was now square onshore, and we would still be on the damned lee shore.

The whole crew was on deck now and we all stood aft by the wheel as Emmett put the skills of a lifetime under sail into coaxing the schooner around the headland. Despite his name, which we made fun of at times, and his predilection for rum, no one could argue the fact that Captain Emmett Cruikshank was a fine seaman. There were things about sailing ships that could only be learned by spending many years before the mast, and Emmett had forgotten more than most of us would ever learn. Crouching over the wheel in his oilskins with his sou'wester pulled low, he squinted ahead, turning only a spoke or two at a time.

He was at his best now, doing what his life so far had trained him for. Over the noise of the wind and the driving spray, I bent towards him and shouted the question that was on everyone's mind.

"Is she going to make it, Emmett?"

His reply was carried away by the wind, but the expression on his face was answer enough for us all.

The schooner's head lifted and fell as each sea came at her. One moment the bowsprit was to windward of the headland and it seemed as if she might make it, then the next moment she would fall away to leeward and the tip of the bowsprit would drift down onto that wicked looking shore.

Emmett had a tricky situation on his hands. The schooner had to be kept going at a decent speed or she would sag down to leeward. To do this, he had to keep the sails full and this meant he had to sail her closer to the shore. On the other hand, he had to keep her off the rocks and this meant that inevitably he was pinching the vessel and slowing her down. Emmett could not afford to err, he had to sail the *Nellie J. King* just right.

The minutes seemed like hours and the hours seemed like a lifetime as the schooner clawed her way to windward along that seemingly endless shore. She picked up tons of green water over the bow when she put her nose into a big one and as she lifted the water rolled aft along the deck in waves.

We were within a half-mile of the land now and the huge white crested breakers appeared as dark mountains to windward of us before they rolled beneath our keel to burst in great explosions of spray on the stark cliffs. I felt as though I was in a giant steel vise, the bulwarks of dark ominous stone close to port and the unyielding seas to starboard, pushing us ever closer. My chest was tight and I found myself clutching the rail with both hands.

Every gust of wind heeled her over so that she buried her lee deadeyes. The decks had long since been washed clean of the coal and the oil drums were gone now too, leaving only a few crates of eggs still lashed atop the main hatch.

The headland drew slowly closer and our schooner fought bravely on. The rocky shore to leeward was so close now that I felt sure we would take the ground at any moment. As each raging mountainous breaker hit the cliffs the spray rose a hundred feet into the air before blowing over the dark ramparts and disappearing inland.

Towards dusk, under an ever-darkening sky, Emmett sailed the *Nellie J. King* past the headland with what was only a few feet to spare. If I had had an apple to throw, I could have hit the shore. Our schooner had sailed a fine race against time, the wind god Aeolus and the great sea, and she had won. Emmett had shown us all a thing or two about how to sail a vessel in heavy weather, but sadly my schooner had fought her last battle. Captain Emmett's memory was not as accurate as he had originally thought, for behind the headland lay no shelter, but yet another long open bay reaching ten or twelve miles to the north-northwest and one more headland.

"I'm sorry, Walt," Emmett said to me sadly his shoulders sagging.

I said nothing to reprimand him. It was obvious that he felt very guilty about our predicament, and in truth it was really not his fault. I gave him a clap on the back and we took stock of our position.

The *King* was sluggish now, her belly full of the seawater seeping in through the many seams that had opened over the last twenty-four hours. The deck pump was clogged with coal dust, and in any case we were too weak with anxiety to try any further. My schooner would weather no more headlands, she would end her days here.

It was a small consolation that the bay to leeward had a sandy shore and the waves seemed to roll in there less violently.

We collected some of our belongings and loaded the two dories before unlashing them from the deck. Jimmy, one of the Mi'kmaqs, put a few crates of eggs into one. We took water in a steel jerrycan, as well as some matches. The land we would have to face was cold and forbidding. A more inhospitable place I had not seen before. I felt strange and weak, but there was no panic. We calmly went about getting the dories ready.

The swell seemed to be less in this bay and at least we would have a chance in the dories. But, my poor old *King* would have no further chances. We let her run off a little towards the shore and when it seemed the right time we let the halyards fly. There was an odd moment as we turned to make up sail, Emmett had to shout at us to leave go and take to the dories.

"There's no time or need for that now, boys," he called to us waving us on as he stood near the boat tackles.

The schooner came to a stop in the middle of the bay about three hundred yards off the beach, and she did us one last service by providing a lee to get off in the dories, which we did without further ado. As we pulled towards the sandy shore I felt a peculiar heaviness of heart, one which over the years I would feel again when faced with a similar loss. She had been my first ship and like a first love, special.

The surf was kind to us and we made the shore without mishap, landing on the beach after only a few minutes. As we unloaded the dories in the growing darkness, I caught a final glimpse of her tall topmasts arcing across the sky and then I saw her no more. Later, as we climbed the hill to find some shelter from the cold onshore wind, I thought I heard her breaking up on the shore. It was not a pretty sound.

Our first night ashore was miserable. Some of the crew knew some woodcraft and built a crude pine-bough shelter where we could escape the wind. We spent the night huddled together trying to keep warm. Thank God we had managed to stay relatively dry and all of us had donned extra clothing before leaving the schooner. We lit a fire, but had no pot to cook the eggs in, so we ate nothing that night. Emmett tried to put a few right in the fire but they exploded.

By daylight, the wind was down and the sun brought with it a degree of warmth. After some debate, Emmett insisted that we strike north along the coast, as he was certain the settlement would be there.

"L'Anse au Loup is there, I know it," he said.

I took a moment and climbed the rise of the hill to see my ship, but she had gone. Only a few splintered timbers remained of her. The dories were still sitting where we had pulled them above the high water mark, but these too would be abandoned as we prepared ourselves for the trek northwards.

We walked throughout the day passing some of the most awe-inspiring landscape I have ever seen. Numerous streams and heavily wooded gullies abounded. The Mi'kmaq lads felt sure there would be many fish in the rivers and game in the woods. I was so cold and tired, however, that I was only interested in getting to the settlement, if indeed there was one. We were all beginning to have doubts. It was disheartening, climbing each hillock hoping the settlement would be on the other side, and finding nothing but wilderness every time.

As evening approached, we wearily climbed to the top of one high bluff, and there at last was the village of L'Anse au Loup, nestled in a small cove, with a dock and three small fishing vessels.

"You see, Walt, I told you it was there." Emmett shouted ecstatically, trying to redeem himself in some small way.

"Yes you did, Emmett. You were right," I replied placing my hand on his shoulder momentarily, a gesture that we were still friends.

With renewed vigour, we started running towards the village shouting as we went. After only a few yards though, we came to an abrupt halt when a pack of huge malamute sled dogs appeared almost out of nowhere to attack us. Snarling and snapping their jaws, they ripped at our clothing. We formed a tight ring and kept our hands high. What a damn stupid way to finish, I thought. We had survived a shipwreck only to end our days as dog meat. Had it not been for the layers of clothing we had on, a number of us would have been badly wounded. Luckily, their barking quickly caught the attention of the villagers and as dusk fell, they came to our rescue.

They were surprised to see us and in some doubt as to the authenticity of our nationalities.

"Where did you come from?" the leader asked suspiciously while keeping us covered with his hunting rifle.

"We were shipwrecked south of here and have walked all day," I explained to him in my most convincing voice, hoping that he would not pull the trigger.

He considered this for a moment, and then after asking a few more questions, accepted our story as the truth. Another of the men collared the dogs, and we gratefully followed them down the hill towards the settlement.

The villagers brought us into their homes and gave us food. These folk showed us a kindness that I will always remember. Their existence was a harsh one, and they had little, yet they gave freely of what they had. I am sure it was no small matter for them to take on additional mouths to feed, but they did not hesitate. We still had some eggs we carried from the boat and we gave them to one of the fishermen's wives. She seemed overly grateful, possibly due to the scarcity of this food.

The families divided us up so that we were spread out and the burden was thus easier to bear. Two of the men from the village retraced our steps in search of our two dories. They brought them back the next morning, having walked and rowed through the night. They were strong men hardened by necessity, for they lived in an unforgiving land. I admired them and gave them the dories as a token of our gratitude and they were very appreciative.

I suffered a disturbing nightmare a few nights later. I dreamt that we caught some of those cruel young German sailors, the ones with the blond hair and cold blue eyes who had looked so callously down the gun barrel at me in the lifeboat. I dreamt we fed them to the malamute dogs. Who knows, had we been a group of shipwrecked German sailors, the villagers might have been less enthusiastic about rescuing us from those beasts.

As we waited for a ship, I went fishing with Jimmy, one of my crew. We procured some fishing line and small hooks from the village and Jimmy tied a few shreds of coloured cloth to a hook with devastating effect. This was especially successful near the mouths of the nearby streams and the fish struck almost every time we cast.

Once, Jimmy and I wandered further than usual from the settlement, and finding a large stream we began to fish. We caught salmon, trout, and char, stringing them on a piece of cod line to carry back to the village. The fish there were big and fat and most obliging. In short time, we caught all that we could comfortably carry back, when, of a sudden Jimmy threw down his line.

"Run," he whispered to me under his breath.

He was looking past me with a terrified look. As I started to question him, I caught a movement out of the corner of my eye and glancing across the stream, and saw a huge bear attempting to cross. I felt that under the circumstances I would not argue the point and the bear was welcome to the fish if he really wanted them. I picked up the long string of fish we had caught and whipped it towards the bear. Without waiting to see if he liked the offering, we took off running as fast as we could. We ran for a good while until we were breathless, and for the first time I outpaced Jimmy, whose legs were longer than mine. We continued to look over our shoulders all the way home. Aside from that one run-in with a bear, I enjoyed the fishing and it benefited the village, as well as the perpetually ravenous malamutes, who devoured the fish as fast as we threw them.

Part of the time, the dogs were kept together in an enclosure and I was surprised at the ferocity of the fights that took place there. The bigger dogs ravaged the smaller ones, stealing their food. How like man they were, I thought. The strong crush the weak and the strong survive even as the weak perish.

One day, Jimmy and I took one of the old *King*'s dories just off shore and half filled it with cod in just a few hours. I was wary though, as the wind had a nasty habit of coming offshore with strength and suddenness. We never ventured too far out. The men of the village all had guns and they shot meat when the diet of fish became too much; there was seal, deer, and birds of numerous varieties.

Despite these diversions, the time went slowly and I felt as though I was in some form of limbo. Finally, some three weeks after we had come ashore, a schooner's spars appeared to seaward. The excitement was catching and we went out with the whole village in their fishing boats to escort the vessel in. I felt elation as we watched her anchor just inside the mouth of the small cove and we went alongside. They were surprised to see us and, as fellow seamen, were saddened to hear of the loss of our ship. They readily agreed to take us aboard and we joined as "additionals" to work our passage to Sydney.

This had been yet another lesson on the realities of a seagoing life, but despite the loss of my ship, I resolved that I would continue. It had been my hope to take the *King* on a voyage south to the islands, but now that was impossible. I said goodbye to Emmett and the crew in Sydney, and I went home once again to Moncton.

The winds of change were blowing and there were events looming over the horizon, which would again shape the course of my life.

On the Ice

THE WAR WAS OVER. The killing had come to an end, but there were far too many mothers whose young sons would never come home. Those thousands of brave young countrymen of mine, whose bones lay scattered across the bottom of the north Atlantic and in forests and fields across the world caused me to contemplate life in a new light. Who can understand war? Its horror is difficult to rationalize and it causes men to become cruel and insensitive.

I felt I had been given a chance to live my life in a way that would be worthwhile, so when it was all over I would be able to say, yes, I spent my days wisely and none were wasted. Something over the horizon pulled me and I felt a great restlessness. I wandered around Halifax searching for an answer. I drank in the bars and listened to the stories of a hundred soldiers and sailors back from the war.

Through a chance meeting in a Halifax tavern, I entered into a partnership with Commander Don McLennon and W.C. McDonald, owner of the Margaree Steamship Company, in a converted minesweeper. Although I suffered a financial loss with the wreck of the *Nellie J. King*, I had, at my father's insistence, carried an insurance policy on the schooner. McLennon and I were young fellows who had met in the beer hall, while McDonald was a mature businessman.

The *Inverleigh* was a decommissioned wooden minesweeper, with an Alpha diesel, which was supposed to push her at twelve knots, but never did. On a good day, we would get about ten knots out of her and so we had to be satisfied with that. She had no sails and sometimes as we chugged along I felt that my old *King* could have run past her. On the other hand, the *Inverleigh*'s engine worked very well and never refused to perform its duty.

We began by putting the vessel into the cargo business with a government contract carrying fish from Yarmouth to Boston, returning with general cargo.

We had difficulty right from the start. There was a tremendous amount of pilferage going on and hundreds of pounds of halibut and cod would disappear. The monthly accounts were always in the red. We were supposed to make one trip per week, but there was so much bad acting on the part of dock unions that we had to take her out of that service. Our last cargo trip was a run to New York with five thousand of Nova Scotia's best Christmas trees, but due to bad weather we didn't arrive until the 29th December, and then we couldn't give them away. Even the dump wouldn't take them, so we ended up standing offshore for a day and a half while we threw them overboard.

Then we tried the sealing business. It was a time when, at least according to our investigations, you could make a good return on sealing and my partners and I decided to give it a try. The harps would come south on the ice in March and April to whelp their young. They came to the Magdalen Islands and surrounding areas in the thousands.

We interviewed a Norwegian captain by the name of Lars Velonson and engaged him as master of the *Inverleigh*. There was also the man known as the sealing master, who would tell the ship's captain where to go for the seals. He was a Newfoundlander and he brought thirty of his countrymen with him who had experience in this business. There were quite a few Newfoundland vessels involved in the sealing trade at the time, so it wasn't hard to find good men.

I sailed on the vessel in the position of mate and we put to sea once again for the coast of Labrador via the Magdalen Islands. Captain Velonson put the *Inverleigh* right alongside the ice and the crew disembarked in groups to search for seal. We leased a small amphibious aircraft that was supposed to be the ticket to our success. It was a strange little plane, with an engine that pushed instead of pulled and it landed and took off from the water. We hired "Bippy," a young American who claimed to be a wartime ace pilot of great experience.

After the ship was secured, we launched it on the starboard side, facing the open water. There was a big perspex hatch and seating for two. Captain Velonson suggested I take the co-pilot's seat and act as spotter, a position I rather reluctantly agreed to. It was to be my first and only flight in the damned thing. Bippy taxied out and opened the throttle, but it seemed to take forever and a day to get into the air and once there, we seemed to struggle to stay up.

"Don't worry, I know how to handle this thang," Bippy shouted to me once we were airborne, but he seemed to be hesitant about which of the numerous buttons and switches to push or pull, and there was one terrifying moment when he mistakenly turned off the engine mid-flight.

His utterance of "sorry" in the air seemed all the louder without the engine noise. Thankfully, he got it re-started and did not dare push that switch again.

We located the seal herds not too far from the vessel and I took notes and bearings for the crew to find them. If success was to be measured by the number of seals killed then we were doing well, for on the next day the men found the largest herds and began to kill them in their hundreds. The ice ran red with blood.

It was bitterly cold as well as dangerous on the ice. The seals were dispatched using the "hackapick," a bat with a sharp spike protruding from the end. This instrument actually had a dual purpose, serving as a safety device as well. If a man fell through the ice or slipped into the sea, there was no way to secure any handhold on the slippery surface and an icy death was usually certain and swift. The hackapick could be used, however, as an ice axe to pull oneself from the water. This simple tool has probably saved many lives.

The new born seals had skulls not yet fully formed and they were killed instantly. The sealers used razor-sharp knives to "sculp" or skin the seals and the hides were stacked in piles to collect later. The men brought seal flippers back to the ship for the cook to prepare. I did not like the taste, however, and had canned sardines instead.

We shifted our position three times over the next few days and moved more to the north along the pack ice. We found more seals, but never again in the numbers we needed. Then the plane crashed. Bippy took off as usual in the morning, but when he had not returned by early afternoon, long after the hour when his fuel should have run out, we became worried. I had long since declined to join him in the little aircraft and as it turned out, with good reason. Our "ace" pilot came walking back along the edge of the ice, just as it began to get dark. He was shivering with cold, but unharmed, except for a cut on his face where the shattered perspex had caught him a blow.

The captain and I, as well as the sealers, gathered round him as he climbed up the rope ladder to the deck of the *Inverleigh*.

"What happened?" I asked him anxiously, helping him over the rail.

"Don't rightly know," he answered casually, stepping aboard. "Motor just kind of stopped."

"Where's the plane?" I asked incredulously.

"Oh, that piece of junk, it hit a piece of ice and sank."

I shook my head in disbelief. This fellow was being far too cavalier about the loss of our aircraft, and for a fleeting moment, I felt like giving him a clout on the ear for being such an ass. On the other hand, I was glad to see that he hadn't been badly injured.

Unfortunately, the plane wasn't insured and would probably render the trip a total financial loss. It did, for without the plane we could find little more seal and the enterprise took on a sour flavour. To top it off, Captain Velonson got us stuck in the ice, where we bent our propeller. We were pulled out by an icebreaker and towed to Sydney, where we had to dry dock the ship for repairs.

After paying off the crew and selling the skins, we were just about even. We had, however, lost the cost of the aircraft, which was over two thousand dollars.

After this, I sold my shares to W.N. McDonald and thankfully got out of the sealing business.

Schooner Tales

OFTEN THERE IS ONE SMALL EVENT OR DECISION which, whilst seemingly unimportant at the time, shapes the rest of one's life. A single action that puts you on the path of your destiny.

After the *Inverleigh* debacle, I found myself in Halifax again. I went to the harbour master's office and after he stamped my sea time, I found I had enough to sit for my master's ticket. In January 1948, I rented a small apartment on Hollis Street and studied for the Board of Trade exam. Luckily, I passed. I was legally a shipmaster now; all I needed was a ship. The cold of winter was receding, and with the promise of summer over the horizon, I resolved to follow my heart and seek livelihood on the sea again.

In April, I read an advert in a newspaper that caught my eye. I read it over a number of times.

"Dude schooners out of Camden," it read. "Come sail on the schooner *Mattie* or *Mercantile* and experience the adventure and romance of life under sail. Weekly cruises leaving from Camden all summer."

It sounded fascinating, so I booked a berth over the phone for a week in June aboard the *Mattie* and later I took the bus down to Camden, Maine.

The seven-day schooner cruise was an intriguing concept. Captain Frank Swift, who owned and operated the business, took tourists out on his two schooners for holiday cruises along the New England coast. The vessels were medium-sized converted fishing schooners, but well painted and clean. Gone were the fish holds, replaced by small four berth cabins and a dining hall. A cook prepared three square meals a day and we slept in clean, if not luxurious, bunks at night.

Hoisting sail each morning, we visited the lovely coves, bays, and small islands so abundant on the coast of Maine. We went swimming in the clear waters and visited picturesque villages and towns. The cook prepared a clam bake
on the shore one evening and a lobster boil another night. My shipmates
seemed eager to experience this way of life, and along with the touristy aspect
of the cruise, many of them actually enjoyed getting involved with the sailing
side of it, hoisting sails or steering.

Although these cruises were a relatively new idea, they seemed to be successful. The sailing along the coast of New England was a pleasure in the summer
and I had a wonderful time. On the third day of my trip, it came to me that this
could be a way in which I could satisfy my own yearnings. The windjammer
cruise business was the answer. A life at sea where guests would pay me to sail
on my ship. Trouble was, I didn't have a schooner any more. I felt a twinge of
sadness; my *Nellie J. King* was only a memory on a rugged Labrador shore. I
did, however, have the money from the shares I sold McDonald in the
Inverleigh, plus the small roll I had saved during the war years.

Returning to Camden after the cruise on the *Mattie*, I spotted a striking
white-hulled topsail schooner moored across the harbour and I asked Captain
Swift who she was.

"Oh, that's the *Yankee*. Irving Johnson sailed her around the world three
times, but now he has a new ship," he told me.

This was enough for me. I walked around the bay and found the owners
puttering about on deck.

"Is she for sale?" I inquired.

"Indeed she is." they replied.

The *Yankee* was a gaff-rigged north sea pilot schooner built of teak in
Germany before the war. She carried a square yard on the foremast setting a
forecourse with a raffee above. A true sailing vessel, the *Yankee* had no engine,
but there was a powerful motor launch, which was put astern to push the
schooner when necessary. At ninety-eight feet and about two hundred tons she
was a stout ship and no doubt very seaworthy. Below, there were berths for sixteen passengers. She had a well equipped galley and a wardroom with a large
gimballed dining table.

The *Yankee* had a nice clipper bow and a pretty, rounded counter stern and
as I stood on her decks there in Camden and felt that she was just what I was
looking for.

I managed to swing a deal a few days later and suddenly I was a ship owner
again. This time, however, I was a certified captain. After a week of outfitting, I

TERRY WAS AN ADVENTURER
LIKE ME, AND BEAUTIFUL TOO.

TERRY WANTED TO KNOW
WHAT LAY AT THE FOREMAST
CROSSTREES — SO SHE CLIMBED
UP TO FIND OUT.

sailed her to Nova Scotia with a delivery crew. Inevitably I suppose, I brought her to the lovely Bras d'Or Lakes, where I had spent so many wonderful months on the old *King*.

The summer of 1948 was kind to us, and the weather stayed warm well into the fall. I began to set up my own cruise business out of Baddeck and there was a good response. I lived on the schooner and when we weren't off on a cruise, the *Yankee* would lay quietly at anchor in the picturesque Baddeck anchorage. When I went ashore in the dory at night, I could look out into the darkness and see her kerosene anchor lantern swinging gently from the forestay. It gave me a good feeling.

The Bras d'Or Lakes are without a doubt one of the most beautiful areas in the world, and the *Yankee* seemed right at home there. Although unaware of it at the time, this was to be the beginning of an important and exciting chapter in my life.

I wasn't the type to go out much, but occasionally I would go with my friend, Joe Francis, to a yacht club or some other social event. One weekend, while in Sydney, I went to a golf club dance with Joe where I met the most wonderful woman I had ever seen. Her name was Terry McNeil and she was as pretty as a picture. She had lovely grey-green eyes and reddish chestnut coloured hair. It was as if I had been hit on the head with a bat. She seemed to be in my every thought and I walked around in a daze. For the first time since I could remember, I was preoccupied with something other than sailing ships. I got my hair cut and I began to comb it more than once a day. I even started putting a little Brilliantine in it.

My crew noticed that I was walking about with quite a spring in my step. I felt great and I looked forward to every opportunity that I could spend with Terry.

Over the next few months we went out as often as possible and I fell in love with her. In Terry I found a kindred spirit. She was an adventurer like me and when I took her out on the schooner for a sail she loved it. A captivating smile enhanced a beautiful personality and I realized I had found the one who would share life's adventures with me.

Inevitably, we married the following year and Terry came to Baddeck to help me run the cruises on the *Yankee*. I was euphoric and felt that life couldn't be sweeter.

The *Yankee* was a famous ship. Under the command of Captain Irving Johnson, she made a number of voyages around the world along the great trade wind routes. He carried paying passengers who acted as crew on the vessel as well. There are those who, captivated by the lure of the sea, are willing to pay for the experience of deep sea voyaging in the traditional way.

Captain Johnson had provided this in the *Yankee*. He was a most competent sailing shipmaster, with the ability to keep the necessary discipline without losing the friendship of the clients he had aboard. A number of people who later made names for themselves sailed with him, such as the movie star Sterling Hayden, who, tired of the phoniness of Hollywood, turned to the sea, and Julie Nicholson, who went on to be an important force in the yacht charter business.

A LAID BACK AFTERNOON ON THE *YANKEE*'S STERN AS WE SAIL THROUGH THE BRAS D'OR LAKES.

I TRIED TO CONVINCE OUR PASSENGERS THAT THE BRAS D'OR WATERS WERE WARM ENOUGH TO ENJOY A DAILY SWIM.

The cruises that Terry and I ran in the Bras d'Or Lakes were based on this concept. The week-long voyages were not luxurious, but were great fun nonetheless. There was comfortable and clean accommodation, with bunks for all on the *Yankee* and the food was fresh and appetizing. There was swimming on the beaches and from the side of the schooner when she was at anchor. We often rigged a gantline from the yardarm and when the vessel was sailing along, some of the more daring passengers would try bosun-chairing, where the rider would swing out away from the vessel in a bosun chair, to trail through the water like a surfer. Every so often, members of our group went ashore to test the scores of rivers and streams surrounding the Bras d'Or Lakes. Trout and salmon were plentiful and the fishing expeditions were always a success. Occasionally, we shot a deer in the woods for the cook to prepare barbeque style on the shore.

We sailed between breakfast and early afternoon. The waters of this beautiful inland-sea were always smooth and the *Yankee* excelled in summer breezes.

SHE GHOSTS ALONG, A WHITE-WINGED VALKYRIE BOUND FOR THE NEXT COVE.

It was the perfect location for the novice, but the magic of a big topsail schooner tacking across the lakes under full sail enamoured the experienced sailors as well. Those so inclined helped hoist the sails or stood a trick at the wheel if they wanted. There was always a picturesque cove to anchor in at the end of the day, while the professional crew would prepare a lobster feast or a clambake.

Our passengers explored local villages and occasionally in light evening airs, the sounds of bagpipes could be heard carrying gently on the wind from some far hill or glen. There were walks and hikes in beautiful park-like surroundings and quiet evenings sitting around shoreside fires. The names of the villages and towns were mostly Scottish and the folk who lived there were friendly clans. Saturday evenings usually found us anchored off Baddeck, where all hands spruced up for the weekend square dance ashore. The *Yankee* cruises became so successful that we received a four-page spread in the *Saturday Evening Post*, and our business was off the to races.

In the spring of the 1949 season we added the sixty-foot Newfoundland schooner *Windbloweth* to the business with a local fisherman to skipper her. She slept an additional six passengers and took care of the overflow from the *Yankee*. She was a pretty little black-hulled schooner, but like many of her cousins she leaked an awful lot. We sold her at the end of the summer, however, after she was rammed in the fog by the steamer *Mudathalapadu*.

There was one great drawback to our new pursuit, which became more and more evident as we progressed: the season was too short. The gorgeous summer weeks just seemed to fly by, and before we knew it, the warm sailing days would come to a close. Even though there seemed to be an abundance of customers who wanted to sail in the summer, there were no passengers to be had for the rest of the year round. Understandably, the cold weather just seemed to take the fun out of it, and for all their popularity, the great Bras d'Or cruises were never destined to be a financial success.

Terry sailed with me until May 1951, when a very small crew member joined us. I was filled with pride when Terry presented me with my first son. He was born at the Mi'kmaq clinic in Baddeck and we named him Robert Louis, but he would always be known as Lou, after Captain Lou Kennedy. He was a fine little boy who cried very little and always seemed to have a good appetite.

When they were not on the ship with me, Terry and Lou lived ashore in the little house we rented in Baddeck, where they would wait for the masts of the *Yankee* to sail in past Beinn Breagh, Alexander Graham Bell's mansion on the hill.

The year 1951 was a successful one and we had more business than we could handle. Terry and I agreed that we needed a second large vessel, and so after

hearing that there was a suitable schooner for sale in the United States, I travelled down to Washington.

I knew as soon as I saw the *Mic Mac* that she was something special. She was a beautiful vessel of 104 feet, built in Shelburne, Nova Scotia for Admiral Raymond, chairman of the Eastern Steamship Company as his private yacht. She had the truest sheerline ever drawn and the proportions of her sleek black hull were

THE SCHOONER *WINDBLOWETH* TAKES THE BREEZE, A BONE IN HER TEETH.

THE *Dubloon*.
SCHOONER MAN QUIP —
WHISTLE FOR A WIND BOYS,
WE'RE NOVA SCOTIA-BOUND!

THE *YANKEE* LEAVES ON ANOTHER CRUISE. BEINN BREAGH IS BEHIND HER HEADSAILS.

perfect. Long, lithe, and lovely with tall slightly raked spars, I fell in love with her immediately and after a brief negotiation I bought her.

More comfortable below decks than the *Yankee*, she was only twelve years old and in excellent condition. She sported no less than four toilets for her six double cabins, so there would be no morning line-ups at the heads. Terry and I had already chosen a new name for the schooner and we called her *Dubloon*.

After a week spent getting ready for sea, I left with a delivery crew of four and started down the Potomac River. After only a few miles, a big white Coast Guard cutter appeared astern rushing frantically towards us and ordering us out of the way. There appeared to be another power vessel behind the Coast Guard cutter, but I could not make her out. A very young officer appeared on the bridge with a loud hailer.

"Captain, move your ship to the side immediately," he instructed me.

I could not move too much because of our very deep draft and I continued on my course in mid channel, causing the young officer great agitation.

"Move your vessel now, captain," he ordered angrily trying to wave us aside.

A few minutes later the presidential yacht, *Sequoia*, with President Truman on the bridge steamed past us. We waved and smiled at each other. The young Coast Guard officer and the cutter disappeared after giving us a rather dirty look.

After a fast but uneventful voyage north along the coast of Nova Scotia, we passed through the St. Peter's Canal into the Bras d'Or Lakes and before long I had her anchored next to the *Yankee* in Baddeck.

Terry and I discussed new possibilities for our cruise business and I began to make a few runs to the French islands of St. Pierre and Miquelon on the *Dubloon*, as she was by far the speedier of the two schooners. The *Yankee* continued her scheduled cruises around the Bras d'Or Lakes under the command of a local schooner captain.

The trips to the French islands were different from our regular cruises and provided our guests with a taste of real ocean sailing. These islands were often shrouded in fog, however, and hard to find. It was difficult to explain to our passengers why we sometimes had to stand off for four or six hours to wait for the fog to clear. Nevertheless, they were only a few days sail from Baddeck, and there was always a good client response. Passengers and crew alike bought rum from the St. Pierre shops to take home, and in the beginning the customs on the Canadian mainland gave us a thorough search whenever we returned.

I knew one customs officer in Sydney, though, with whom I rekindled an old relationship. It was based upon an agreement we reached when I was running the old *Nellie J. King* up to St. Pierre. He always made it his business to be the one who inspected the *Dubloon* and I always had his rum ready. Coming aboard as soon as we docked, we would quickly go below where we had our standard conversation. It was always short and went something like this.

"Morning skipper, have a good trip?"

"Yup, can't complain."

"Got anything to declare?"

"No, not really, just a bottle or two of rum."

"I got to be really on the ball these days, all kinds of smuggling going on. Got my rum?" He would say these words exactly the same way each time.

"Oh yes, got it right here," I always answered.

The prescribed two bottles of rum were then passed over and my friend wouldn't bother to look for the other ten cases, which we had stowed in the bilges. It was a real gentlemen's agreement and, I thought, downright sporting.

I bought my cargoes of rum from the Folquet brothers of St. Pierre and we became good friends. They owned the liquor warehouses there and were fea-

THERE WERE LOTS OF HIDDEN COVES WHERE WE COULD
GO ASHORE UNNOTICED.

tured in the book, *The Real McCoy*, by the famous rum-runner, Captain McCoy of the schooner *Arethusa*. They invited me to their home for dinner when the *Dubloon* was in port and showed me a copy of McCoy's book with the following inscription on the front page:

"From Captain McCoy of the schooner *Arethusa*. In all my dealings with thieves and vagabonds I have met none finer than the Folquet brothers."

When I didn't clear into Sydney, I managed to land my liquor somewhere else in one of the hundreds of other coves and bays along the coast. Not to slur the authorities, but they just did not have the local knowledge to catch me. I knew the coastline like the back of my hand and I had a fine swift schooner. I did not feel at all guilty about our little extracurricular cargoes. If a few decent citizens got to uncork some unadulterated rum once in a while, then that was damned good.

LITTLE LOU LOOKS A LITTLE UNCERTAIN ABOUT OUR PLANNED VOYAGE SOUTH.

Terry was appalled the first time I arrived back in Sydney and filled the trunk of her car with cases of liquor. As she drove home that night alone, she noticed a mountie trailing her and she was terrified. It was only a coincidence though and the McNeil clan enjoyed a few glasses of the liquor over the next few months.

Fall arrived and, as if by magic, the clients for our two schooners disappeared. The Bras d'Or cruises were over for the year and the trips to the French islands came to an end. It was alright making a few extra dollars profit carrying rum when you had passengers on board, but it would look mighty suspicious running dude schooner cruises in the winter with no dudes aboard. My answers lay far to the south.

Earlier that summer, Terry and I had experimented by placing advertisements in the American papers for winter cruises in the West Indies and Bahamas, based out of Miami. The response had been encouraging and so we made the decision to try it out. Mooring the *Yankee* in a cove close to Baddeck, we left one of our regular crew in charge of her. Then Terry, little Lou, and myself took a crew of five to sail the *Dubloon* south to Florida. It was the fall of 1951.

It was a rough trip initially, and Lou was very seasick. I felt pretty sorry for the little fellow as he lay in the bunk with the dry heaves. He was making the most horrible noises, but didn't cry and Terry held him while he was awake. He didn't eat for almost two days and I began to worry that I may have taken him to sea too early. Then, surprisingly, he just got over it and was never sick again. I perched him in the main sheet coil on the lee side of the cockpit and he was happy as could be.

I took a measure of my schooner as soon as we were east of the Gulf Stream and we cracked on all sail. The *Dubloon* did not let me down; she was as fast as the wind and we raced south like a bird on the wing.

Arriving in Miami, we berthed at Pier 5 and began preparations for the winter charter cruises. There was much to do and we spent hours sanding and painting the topsides and re-varnishing the teak bright work. Later, we took the schooner up the Miami River to the Merrill Stevens Shipyard for a week of mechanical maintenance.

Visiting the Seminole Indians further up stream, we watched them wrestling with alligators for the tourists in a large pit. I would always take a second look whenever one of the log-like reptiles drifted past the moored schooner on the surface, and I wondered what would have happened if one of us had fallen overboard. Luckily no one ever did and I never found out.

Terry and Lou stayed aboard until the last minute, when I had to put them ashore in a rented cottage in Key Biscayne. We needed the bunks for the paying passengers.

It was January 1952 and the first Caribbean cruise of the schooner *Dubloon* would take her on an adventure through many islands in the Bahamas and then down through the Windward Passage to Cape Haitian in Haiti. We would visit Port au Prince and then circle back to Miami via the Cayman Islands and Havana, Cuba. I planned the voyage to last five weeks.

The ship was ready to put to sea and all of the twelve passengers on the list were aboard except one. Count Christopher Gabrowsky, a man of some professed sailing experience, was late. The deadline for sailing was drawing near and there was still no sign of him, when at the last minute a taxi came screeching to a halt near the dock and the count got out. He was a tall, aristocratic chap with a goatee. He sent his driver down to tell the crew to come and carry his baggage. It had been clearly explained in the brochure that baggage be kept to one duffel bag. Our count arrived with a grand total of five suitcases and a large sea bag. I began to wonder if this one was going to be trouble.

Evening found us putting to sea, and by eight we had sunk the lights of

Miami astern. The Gulf Stream can be rough and that night it was bumpy and windy, but the watches were progressing well and the schooner was making a good time of it and sailing fast. The trouble began during the mate's watch, when I was kept awake by the thundering of the sails every few minutes. I went up on deck and saw the count at the wheel and doing a poor job of it. He had been given a compass course, but seemed unable to hold it. Before I could say anything, the count explained, "Captain, this vessel is not properly balanced." Of course there was nothing wrong with the schooner's balance, he was steering way up into the wind and then down again, so much that a snake would have had difficulty following us.

"You've got to keep her on course," I told him, but he was not in any mood to accept that he was the cause of the problem.

We had words and I relieved the count, giving the helm to the mate. After telling him to hold her a bit better, I went back down to my bunk.

The run across the Gulf Stream is not a long one and by daylight we were coasting along by Bimini, before going through the pass at Gun Cay. The weather was announcing there was a northern on the way, so I decided to take the *Dubloon* to Cat Cay where there was more shelter.

Cat Cay was a rich man's hideaway frequented by the famous big game fisherman of the day, and it was a very expensive place. Everything had to be brought in by boat and so prices for fuel and provisions were usually beyond the reach of the ordinary cruising sailor, and the likes of me. I had anchored there before, but had never visited the exclusive Cat Cay Club. Non-members were not encouraged to drop by.

Cat Cay was also a port of entry for the Bahamas and so after we were anchored, I went ashore in the dingy to present the ship's papers and crew lists to the local authorities. The rest of the crew and passengers were not allowed ashore until the ship was properly cleared.

Walking back towards the schooner to let our guests know they could now go ashore, who did I bump into but the count strolling along the waterfront.

"You know you weren't supposed to come ashore until after the ship was cleared," I told him, trying to keep my temper in check.

"Don't concern yourself captain, I'm very well known here," he assured me. "In fact, I'm just on my way to the Cat Cay Club for a drink."

I was surprised, as few people could just casually drop in to the club, but he reassured me yet again that everyone knew him around here. I then made the big mistake of agreeing to join him for a drink there. I wondered if he was trying to make up for the night before.

I returned to the ship and told the other passengers they could go ashore. Then I joined the count again and we strolled for awhile, admiring the lovely homes before finally coming to an area of beautifully manicured lawns and gardens, leading up to a very posh-looking building. On the gate there was the usual hanging plaque with a cat painted on it, along with a big golden cay underneath.

Crossing the perfect lawn, we came to an umbrella-clad table with chairs, and sat down. Moments later an older lady in a flowered dress approached us, and with a pleasant English accent bade us a good day.

"May I help you?" she asked politely.

The count introduced himself and asked for a whisky and soda and I ordered a beer. Looking a little confused, she walked away and brought our drinks a few minutes later.

We were ready to order our second round, but when Count Gabrowsky signalled to the lady, she turned away instead and disappeared inside the main building. A moment later she came walking back over to us with a rather distinguished-looking gentleman at her side. The elderly man smiled at us and inquired graciously, "Is there something my wife and I can do for you?"

"Well, we're ready for another round, and then I'd like to show my friend inside the Cat Cay Club," the count said pointing towards the main building.

The old gentleman smiled again. "Well, I am Admiral Smith-Jones and this is my wife, Sarah. I'm afraid this is not the Cat Cay Club, it's our home. The Cat Cay is just over the way."

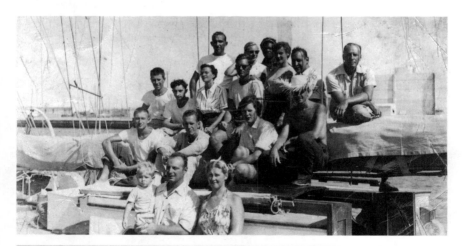

TERRY AND LOU JOIN THE CREW FOR OUR SECOND CARIBBEAN CRUISE.

I have never been so embarrassed in my life and even the count seemed to be caught with his sails aback. Needless to say, we left straight away. I offered to pay for the drinks, but the admiral would not hear of it, and I thought he took the invasion in good spirit.

As for Count Gabrowsky, he continued to be a royal pain in the neck and there was no way I could have put up with him for five weeks. Thankfully, he left the ship in Nassau and that was the last I ever saw of him. I was told some years later that he just disappeared at sea on his sloop, without a trace.

We arrived back in Miami five weeks later and I was happily reunited with my family. Our first Caribbean cruise had been a great success.

The day after our return, as I was running ashore in the small launch, I saw a big square topsail schooner anchored near to us off Bay Front Park. I circled a couple of times admiring her and saw the golden letters spelling *"Caribee"* emblazoned across her stern. Little did I know that our paths would soon cross again.

Our next voyage was scheduled to depart in a few days. We were not fully booked this trip, so I saw no reason why Terry and Lou could not come along this time. So, we closed up the little house in Key Biscayne and they moved aboard the *Dubloon*.

NEDDY LAUNCHES A REBUILT
SURF BOAT ON A CALMER DAY
AS THE *DUBLOON* STANDS OFF
TO WAIT FOR US.

We sailed for parts further south this time and somehow I felt that I was in the place I had been destined to find. The great trade winds filled our canvas and the blue Caribbean sea rolled gently under the keel. I had never felt happier in my life and Terry felt the same.

The *Dubloon* sailed across the Anegada Passage and towards the Rock of Saba, which rose precipitously from the sea. A ruggedly high volcanic island just south of the Virgin Islands, Saba is very similar to Pitcairn Island in the Pacific. There is no natural harbour and the only way to get ashore was in the renowned "surf boat," a rather decrepit longboat operated by the famous Neddy Van Wart.

Neddy had built himself a reputation over the years for being able to land his legendary surfboat on Saba in almost any weather conditions. While in St. Thomas, I had been told to just heave to close in the lee and Neddy would come out and take my passengers ashore—for a reasonable price, of course.

As luck would have it, we were to attempt our first landing on Saba when there was a good surf running, but also at a time when the great Neddy has been into the strong white rum the islanders call "Jack Iron."

When he came out to the *Dubloon* to pick us up, he seemed to be doing a lot of weaving and falling around in the boat, but I put it down to the waves. In any event Terry, with Lou in her arms, and I climbed into the surfboat, along with eight of the passengers and we headed for the shore. The schooner would jog in the lee under the command of the mate until we returned.

Now Neddy had gained fame by being able to sense the ideal moment to launch his surfboat between waves into the little landing slot on the rocky shore. That day, however, it seemed as if Neddy waited for the biggest swell of all to come along before urging his two oarsmen forward. The boat careened in on the crest of a huge wave and hit the rocky shore with such force that its bow split wide open, leaving us all awash at the water's edge.

We nearly lost little Lou then, as the undertow tried to suck him out to sea. Terry, however, was a strong woman and she grabbed him by the foot, while I grabbed her by the arm, dragging them both ashore. Neddy and his two oarsmen scrambled up to the edge of the surf line and stood next to us. Neddy seemed to be at a loss as to how this could have occurred.

"Oh Lard, how dis could happen to me, nuh?" he asked stunned.

One of his crew, a stout serious-looking man, who had no such difficulty in determining the cause of the accident turned to his skipper.

"Neddy, you damn jackass, ah did tell you leave de rum dis marnin."

Even though we had a rather unceremonious landing on the island of Saba, I felt it was only right to pay for our trip ashore, and after leaving a very dejected Neddy, we began to explore the island. We were pretty wet, but the tropical sun soon dried our clothes as we hiked to the town at the top of Saba rock, which for some unknown reason was called "Bottom." Terry bought some pieces of the Saba lace that the Dutch women there are famous for.

Later, the bosun from the schooner rowed in to collect us in the ship's dory, and did a better job of it than Neddy, who was still there picking up the pieces of his surfboat along the shore.

Later, we sailed to Kingston, Jamaica, where we hired a plump local woman to babysit Lou for a day on the schooner. She fell in love with him, and when it came for time for us to sail she cried and begged to come with us. Melvina became a part of our family that day and stayed with us for a number of years as we wandered the islands.

The winter season proved to be a busy one and the *Dubloon* made some fast passages in the stiff winter breezes. I was impressed and encouraged by the number of clients who came to sail with us. Although most had no sailing experience, all were nonetheless captivated, as our schooner—canvas taut—revelled in the brisk trade winds. It was the lure of the sea. Eons ago we had come from this briny mixture, and perhaps there is a connection that cannot be severed entirely. Perhaps the warm caress of the deep blue Caribbean as it rolled gently beneath our keel stirred feelings irresistible, from times long past.

As the winter season came to a successful conclusion, we prepared to return to Cape Breton for the summer. Terry and I decided that she would drive to Nova Scotia with Lou and Melvina, as the voyage north that time of year could prove rough. We purchased a second-hand Ford car, and the three of them headed back to the little house in Baddeck.

Shortly afterwards, I set sail with a crew of five for Nova Scotia, intending to put our two schooners to work for the summer in the Bras d'Or Lakes. The voyage was uneventful until we began to experience some engine trouble half-way up the eastern seaboard. I believe we picked up some dirty fuel in Miami and it was choking the injectors of the main engine. We stopped in City Island, New York, for some repairs and also to wait out some weather. The marina engineers removed the injectors from the main engine and took them to the workshop for repair. That evening, the weather deteriorated and my schooner was trapped at the marina dock. I tried to find someone to help us, but it was Friday night and the marina office was closed.

As the wind rose the *Dubloon* ground herself against the rough, heavy timbered wharf. I was unable to move her to a safer berth because there were no injectors in the main engine and the marina engineers were nowhere to be found. By the early hours, quite a surge had built up, pounding the schooner against the dock. We tried to tend her lines and fenders, but it was futile.

Finally, we were forced to take refuge in a nearby warehouse, and I watched through the night as *Dubloon* wounded herself. I felt as though I was the one taking the beating.

A grey dawn broke and the storm passed as quickly as it had come. I felt sick as I stood on the dock looking at my schooner. Her port bow was damaged and twenty feet of her bulwark on that side was stove in. Her long bowsprit was broken at the stem. I wandered along her decks seeking some sort of an explanation. It had all happened so fast and so arbitrarily. The vibrancy and life which had emanated from her wooden planks as she romped the ocean waves was gone now. She would need considerable work before she could spread her wings again. I felt angry, and had I known then what I know now, I would have sued the pants off the marina.

Then came a piece of really shocking news. Terry called me from Baddeck to tell me that the *Yankee* had sunk during the winter under very mysterious circumstances. I made arrangements with a nervous marina manager to berth the *Dubloon* at City Island, until I could either repair her or sell her. They seemed overly anxious to cooperate and agreed to do this free of charge. I suspect that the man realized his culpability in the damaged schooner laying on his dock.

I took the bus north and pondered the strange vagaries of life. Arriving in Baddeck, I began to investigate the loss of the *Yankee*.

Events surrounding her sinking seemed to be very suspicious, but no one could confirm what had really happened. It was pretty common knowledge that the ballast in her gimballed dining table held lead ingots, which Irving Johnson dove up from the wreck of the *HMS Bounty* at Pitcairn Island. There were rumours that some people from Halifax had expressed a big interest in this.

The schooner had been vandalized and stripped of fittings and gear. The top of the teak main hatch had been ripped off, so the dining table could be removed. That could have been the reason for the ship being broken into, but why sink her afterwards?

I braved the cold water and dove down on her with a mask and snorkel. She was only a few feet below the surface and I was able to see into her very easily. I noticed that some of the sea cocks were broken off and opened, lending more suspicion. To this very day, she still lies in a pretty pine tree lined Baddeck cove, a mystery still unsolved.

With the loss of the *Yankee* in Cape Breton and the *Dubloon* being damaged during the storm at City Island, New York, we had sustained a heavy blow both financially and psychologically. We continued to live at our little house in Baddeck, but we had no schooner with which to run our summer cruises.

The summer weeks passed and we decided to sell the *Dubloon*. An East Coast yachtsman made a good offer and he contracted the same City Island yard to repair her. I had made some wonderful passages in the *Dubloon* and whenever I think of her, I sense a moistness in my eye and a special feeling that is reserved for something dear to one's heart.

There develops a unique bond between a man and his sailing ship that is not unlike that between a man and a woman. A special pride when her bow lifts unbidden to meet the oncoming sea or when she makes an especially fast run. Only those who have stood beneath the foresail boom on a starlit night and heard the magic of the ocean as it washes away to leeward can truly appreciate these feelings. I loved each and every one of my ships over the years and grieved when we parted company.

We tried to locate another suitable schooner for our business, but this was proving difficult. While there were a number of vessels on the market, most were far beyond my financial means. However, we continued to look, buying yachting magazines and making weekly telephone calls to the various yacht brokers.

One day, I received a call from an agent in Florida indicating that the schooner *Caribee* was for sale. She was laying at the Merrill Stevens Shipyard on the Miami River. I remembered admiring her at anchor off Biscayne Park the previous year. This piece of encouraging news was followed by something even more wonderful, for at that time Terry gave birth to a little girl. We named her Janeen.

The owner of the *Caribee* was a wealthy young man by the name of Richard B. Church, who had bought the schooner for a world cruise he had planned for his new bride. However, when he showed her the ship she refused even to set foot on it. She wanted a chrome plated gin palace, not an old clipper ship. The *Caribee* at that moment held little value for Mr. Church.

The *Caribee* was not an old ship though. She was a replica of the famous Baltimore clipper types and only a few years old. In fact, she was an amalgam of all the better characteristics of that type, while being less extreme. This meant that her design was better for all round sailing, as opposed to being built solely for speed. She was less lofty in the rig and her hull sections were fuller in the bilge and she had perhaps a bit more freeboard and sheer than her cousins. She was designed by Howard Chapelle, a leading authority on period vessels, and built by William Albert Robinson, a famous seafarer in his own right.

Mr. Church lived in King's Point, Long Island, and I called him by phone and talked to him about buying his schooner. The result of this conversation was that I was invited to his mansion. And so, I left Terry and the expanding Boudreau clan in Baddeck and made my way to New York. I was feeling pretty uncertain of myself as I got off the bus, but Mr. Church was there to meet me in his Jaguar and we drove to the shores of Long Island.

At his home we started to exchange life stories over a steady supply of strong rum and cokes brought on a silver tray by a uniformed maid. At dinner time, we stopped drinking long enough to have a quick meal, but resumed in earnest immediately afterwards. I believe I managed to gain Mr. Church's sympathy for my recent misfortunes, with the result that later that night he agreed to sell the *Caribee* to me for $7,500.

The next morning we drove to his lawyer's office and I passed over the $4,000 in cash I had been carrying in my pocket. The balance was payable as I earned it. Declining Mr. Church's offer of another evening of fine rum and tales, I duly signed the papers and took off before he could change his mind.

Arriving in Miami at two in the morning, with little cash left after the bus fare, I walked tiredly to the shipyard, but found it locked. Failing to raise a night watchman, I made my way down to Bayfront Park, where all the unfortunates hung out, sleeping on the benches. It was a balmy night and I soon found a guy willing to give up half of his bench and a few pages of the *Miami Herald* newspaper he was sleeping under. I fell asleep right there, a happy and content man again.

The next morning, my bench-mate was still there and we both sat up at the same time. He looked over at me and grinned slightly as he took the near empty bottle of "Ruby Red" from the paper bag under the bench.

THE *CARIBEE* WAS OUR HOME AS WE WANDERED THE ISLANDS.

"What you doin' in Miami then?" he asked with bleary eyes.

Without really thinking I answered honestly, "I'm here to pick up my yacht."

My vagrant friend burst out laughing, and getting up he yelled over to his buddies on the other benches.

"Hey guys, this nut here thinks he going to pick up his yacht today," and they all laughed some more.

I saw the funny side of it too, and when I noticed my rumpled clothes and stubble on my chin, I laughed till my sides hurt.

At eight o'clock, I walked back to the shipyard and stepped aboard the *Caribee* as her proud new owner. My ship felt strong and heavy beneath my feet, and although there were few dollars left to my name, I couldn't stop smiling.

I spent the day exploring the ship and I was not disappointed. She was a fine vessel and I could see that her builder had used only the best materials in her construction. Her heavy ninety-eight-foot hull was planked with African apitong, a reliable hardwood, and her decks and brightwork were all teak. She had the traditional clipper rake to her spars and two square yards hung on the foremast. The *Caribee* had a swift look; a long sweeping black hull, topped with white bulwarks punctuated with black gunports. Her name was carved across her broad transom, set above the golden bust of a Creole woman. She had a real brass twelve-pound naval cannon amidships, on a teak gun carriage with all the tackles. Under her bowsprit there was a female figurehead depicting her namesake.

Terry, Melvina, Janeen, and Lou packed up and drove the old blue Ford back down to Miami and arrived safely after a long and tiring journey. I moved the *Caribee* to the anchorage in Bayfront Park and began to put a crew together. Soon, we were ready to take her out for a sea trial, but there was one thing I had to do first.

I took the launch ashore to the marina convenience store and bought some fresh bread, salami, and a few bottles of wine. The *Caribee* was anchored only two hundred feet or so from the park seawall and when I got back aboard, I blew the fog horn several times and waved to the vagrants in the park, who came over to see what was going on. I got into the launch and brought over the wine and food, giving it to the grizzled-looking friend who had been kind enough to share his bench and newspaper with me.

"Hey look fellas, it's the new bum and his yacht," he said in amazement.

I learned over the following weeks that there was a rags to riches tale being told along the waterfront about this Canadian bum who struck it lucky and now owned a big fancy yacht. And so developed the unusual relationship between the vagrants of Bayfront Park and the schooner *Caribee*. When I left on a cruise, they would wave me goodbye and when I returned they would cheer me to the anchorage. Whenever there was anything extra, I brought it in to them and we remained friends.

The days of sailing back to Nova Scotia in the spring were over. There was more than enough business to keep us in these southern latitudes now and although I would forever hold dear my ties to the north, the memory of that cold fog-bound coast had already begun to recede. The warm trade winds blew all year round here and would, over the coming years, bring the *Caribee* and our family to new and exotic places. Terry and the little ones sailed with me whenever there was a free cabin, and during the times they had to stay ashore, they waited in the little cottage in Key Biscayne for our raked spars to loom over the horizon.

In the beginning, there were ten-day cruises to the Bahamas with college students and other people in search of adventure. The Bahamas were perfect for this type of cruising and the hundreds of Robinson Crusoe-esque bays, cays, and islets lent themselves well to our cause. We were the first to operate this type of cruise here and we based them on our successes in the Bras d'Or Lakes. Setting up agents in many of the major universities around the United States, we enjoyed a tremendous response. It was not long before the cruises went further afield and for longer periods of time.

My second son, Peter, chose Miami as the port of his arrival. He was born

A SHALLOW CORAL REEF LURKED JUST BELOW THE SURFACE OF A SEEMINGLY BENIGN TROPICAL SEA, AND I HAD TO NAVIGATE CAREFULLY.

in December 1954, and I was once again a proud father. Terry had brought two children into the world in one year. We joked privately that if things continued so, we would soon have sufficient numbers to put together a complete schooner crew.

The *Caribee* sailed on, spreading her wings across the Great Bahama Bank ever southwards, across the Anegada Passage to new ports of call. Somehow I knew that another new chapter had been opened in our lives, and that over the horizon further to the south, there were great things waiting for us. I was truly blessed, for what more can a man ask for in this life than a loving wife, a fine schooner, and the smiles of his children at his feet.

Islands of the
Trade Winds

IN THE TIME WE CAME TO KNOW MOST of the islands to the south, the *Caribee* in turn became a well-known vessel in those parts. We sailed to the Bahamas, Cuba, Hispanola, Puerto Rico, Jamaica, Cayman Islands, Virgin Islands, the Leewards, and the Windwards. All of these places were different, with rich and contrasting histories, and their peoples were as diverse as the lands from which they had first hailed. The common thread was that wherever they had come from, they had travelled over the sea. There were descendants of Dutch sailors on Saba and the ancestors of the British and Scottish whalers on Bequia. By far the largest ethnic groups in the islands, however, were the descendants of African slaves brought there many years ago.

It interested me that the people of St. Lucia and Martinique had evolved so differently. These islands were barely twenty miles apart, but while the African heritage in St. Lucia had remained strong, with little mixing of the races, many of the people of Martinique were a result of the inter-racial unions that were more common there. Apparently, the French planters had been less prudish than their British counterparts on the island next door.

All of the islands had fresh produce markets and Terry and I delighted in shopping there, learning the names of all the new tropical fruits and vegetables and how to cook and prepare them. Mangoes, breadfruit, soursop, sugar-apple, mamy-apple, golden apple (there were many different types of apple fruit), and cosol: we enjoyed them all. Colourfully attired island women with Madras headpieces shouted the virtues of their wares from wooden stalls as they tried to entice buyers.

The local fish markets were colourful as well, and the daily catch was usually displayed and sold before noon, as there was no refrigeration. There was often whale meat on display, especially in the island of Bequia where the local men held precariously to the age-old tradition of whaling. The flesh was almost black and I was never of a mind to try it.

The Bahamian islands were limiting to us because of the shallow waters, and the islands themselves were very flat. Truth be told I put the *Caribee* aground a couple of times, but I was always able to get her off again. More often than not we had to anchor the schooner a mile or so from the shore.

But the fish! Oh the delights of the lobster and seafood. In those days there was a seemingly endless supply of both, as well as conch. One of my crew was a Bahamian called Fletch, a fisherman from Nassau, who kept us in fresh seafood on our island trips. He was a strong, muscular man with a ready smile and a most capable seaman. I grew to like Fletch immensely, he was a great asset to the ship and had an unsinkably cheery disposition. He was always humming or singing an old Calypso song, the first few lines of which went like this:

Rose an Dina,
Rosita an Clemintina,
Down by de cornah posing,
Bet your life is somting dey sellin

Armed with his rubber-powered speargun, Fletch dove down to the coral reef and took a heavy toll on the lobster population. He was always able to shoot a big fat grouper or red snapper if we needed one for dinner. Fletch dove up conches well, those huge molluscs that lived in the turtle grass, and "Cooky" would prepare the best conch chowders ever.

I learned to free dive too and it was a revelation to me. There was another exotic world beneath the surface; one of magic crystal clear water and vivid colours. The coral reefs of the West Indies are like undersea gardens, with multi-hued sea fans and corals of a dozen types and shades. I had never seen such a wide variety of fish life. There must have been a hundred different types varying in size, shape, and colour. Parrot fish of many different hues and shapes roamed the reef, feeding on the coral surfaces with their protruding beaks. Angelfish, sand divers, moray eels, and light grey spadefish wandered the coral heads in search of their particular foods. Big silvery sided horseye jacks and the occasional heavier amberjack cruised the edge of the reef, where it dropped off into deeper water. Schools of sardine hovered in the thousands near the surface, providing sustenance for the various predatory species. Red snappers were abundant too. In a seemingly nonchalant manner they roamed the edge of the reef looking for prey. They would cruise over the sandy patches and take shrimp and small crabs. These fish were amongst the tastiest of them all.

Fletch was a master of the undersea hunt. Whenever we needed a large fish for dinner he would happily oblige, but there was more to it than met the eye. It was not just a matter of diving a few feet down and harpooning a large grouper as it sat watching you. Fletch sometimes went down to depths of more than eighty feet with his mask and fins. There was great technique in successful grouper hunting and Fletch had developed this into an art.

"You got to move real slow," he told me, "swim jus' like a fish, or de grouper goin' run."

I attempted to follow his instructions, but never came close to matching Fletch's underwater skills.

There were the ever-curious barracudas, which seemed to appear as if by magic whenever we entered the water. Long ominous-looking predators with silver streamlined bodies, their jaws were filled with razor sharp teeth. They had a habit of hovering a few feet behind us while moving their jaws slowly, as if "smacking their lips." I learned that this was just the method they used to pass oxygen over their gills, and not a threatening gesture. Occasionally, a very large specimen would make us feel uneasy with its unwanted attention and we would move to another area, but there would usually be another barracuda waiting there. Once, moments after I had just speared a good sized red snapper, one brazen fellow rushed in and took it off the end of my spear. I didn't argue the point, graciously letting the barracuda have the fish. Despite their menacing looks, however, none ever made a deliberate attack on any of my crew or passengers.

In later years, I became friends with Dave Ferneding, a seafaring colleague, and the only man I ever met who had been attacked by a barracuda. He had been a U.S. Navy diver at the time, taking photographs below a damaged U.S. destroyer in a Mexican harbour. The water had been very murky and he was wearing a black wet suit. The huge barracuda had come in fast and hit the shiny camera he was holding in front of him. Dave retains some nasty looking scars on his stomach as a result of this incident, but he is always the first to point out that the attack was almost certainly a case of mistaken identity. Nevertheless, the large silversided torpedoes with the jagged teeth always made me nervous and I never got used to having them around.

Huge schools of silversides drifted above the Bahamian reefs in shimmering shifting clouds, like jewels adrift in the current. The water was so clear in many areas that we could see down a hundred feet or more and one had the sensation of flying over the sea bottom. The corals were diverse in colour and shape as well. We swam over brain corals the size of small cars, so named because of their resemblance to the human brain, while nearer to the surface antlerhorn corals spread their wide flat branches.

Every once in a while, one of our group would get careless and come into contact with the black spiny sea urchins that littered the reef. They would come back to the schooner with the mildly poisonous barbs embedded in their feet or hands. I always enjoyed watching the expressions on our guests' faces when Fletch offered the local remedy.

"What can I do to get them out?" asked the unsuspecting victim, never dreaming of Fletch's cure.

"You got to pee on it. You want me to…?" was Fletch's standard offer. Strangely enough, this bizarre remedy seemed to work, helping to dissolve the tiny black barbs. Despite the barracudas and sea urchins, the *Caribee*'s guests loved snorkelling on the reef and so did I.

The open channels between the islands held schools of fish of many diverse species. We learned to pull trolling lines as the schooner sailed along. The lines were heavy monofiliment—a type of transparent fishing line—of perhaps three hundred pounds test, and we would attach them to the taffrail on the stern. Fletch showed us how to rig the yellow feather baits in order to attract the fish, and as we sailed along we caught tuna, wahoo, dorado, kingfish, barracuda, and a half dozen other species. All were excellent eating, especially when served up fresh an hour later.

We occasionally caught sharks, more so in the Bahamas, but I steadfastly refused to eat them, despite Fletch's urgings. I joked that I had made a pact with the species many years prior; they would not eat me and I would not eat them.

One afternoon, while sailing slowly along off Frazer's Hog Cay in the Berry Islands, I spotted a large shark trailing the schooner. It was one of those long hot Bahamian days, when there was little wind and the *Caribee* seemed almost suspended on a calm sea. The tropical sun beat down from an azure sky and the decks were almost too hot to walk on. We were moving along at only two or three knots, when I saw the grey fin break surface thirty feet astern of the schooner. I decided to try and catch the beast and calling Fletch, pointed out past the stern. He saw it right away.

"Dat's a big one, Cap," he exclaimed smiling broadly.

"Well, get the shark line and let's see if we can take him," I said.

It always made for an exciting event to haul one of these voracious creatures aboard and our passengers would often seem thrilled and terrified at the same time.

Fletch came walking aft with the shark gear and began to sort it out on the deck. It consisted of a long coil of half-inch line, connected to twenty feet of small chain attached to a hook. The hook was ten inches long, ending in a wicked curve with a barb.

"What have you got for bait?" I asked him.

"Cooky give me a fish head, Cap," he replied holding it up for all to see.

It was the head of a tuna the cook had just dressed out for dinner, and it must have weighed all of ten pounds. Fletch slid the big hook into the eye, tying it on with some heavy twine. He then held his handy work up for me to inspect.

"Sweet bait, ain't it, Cap," he said. Fletch didn't like sharks, so he took pleasure in catching the devils.

The shark was still swimming sinuously astern of us and we could see the sun shimmering off his grey-blue back.

"Yes, you greedy buggah, we goin see if you hungry now," Fletch said as he threw the baited hook over the taffrail.

Slacking out about thirty feet of line, he made it fast to the main sheet bit on the stern. It didn't take the shark a moment to find the big tuna head, and those of us standing on the stern watched as the brute came up slowly, opened his cavernous mouth and swallowed the bait. The big hook immediately sunk into the shark's upper jaw, and suddenly all hell broke loose. The big fish began fighting like a demon when he realized something was wrong. At first, he thrashed around on the surface, throwing up huge splashes of spray. Then he sank down, sulking at the extent of the line as if trying to return to the depths from which he had come. But he was well hooked, and as we watched his efforts to escape from the stern of the *Caribee*, it became clear that he was slowly tiring. We let the great fish play itself out for awhile, swimming from side to side and as deep as the line would allow. We had a good look at him as he turned broadside, and I realized that we had hooked ourselves a very large beast. After perhaps twenty minutes of fighting, he seemed to tire and Fletch had the guests line up on the aft deck ready to haul on the line when he untied it from the bit.

"Y'all ready all you self now, and when ah tell you pull, you pull like hell," he instructed.

The dozen or so passengers answered in the affirmative and Fletch threw the line off the bit. Everyone was surprised at the weight as they struggled to turn the fish. For a moment, it was a question of who was pulling who. After a few minutes of grunting and several good shouts of "heave, and heave together," they began to win and the big shark slowly started coming in.

I went below to my cabin, and taking the Smith and Wesson .38 calibre revolver from the drawer beneath my bunk, I loaded the six chambers. I did not want the shark too lively when we brought it aboard.

With Fletch supervising, our passengers hauled the shark alongside. As it lay there with its snout out of the water, I leaned over the rail and shot it six times in the top of the head. It thrashed around in its death throes, thumping the ship's quarter with its tail, until finally it lay still. Fletch rigged the gantline from the main mast to the shark chain and we hoisted it aboard.

It was a tiger shark, some fourteen feet in length and the biggest I had ever seen. The species is distinguishable from others by its wide square snout and crooked teeth. We hung it amidships by its upper lip for all to see, lashing it to the starboard rigging. One of the passengers got out a measuring tape to check the spread of its jaws. They gapped some twenty-eight inches top to bottom and by thirty-three inches wide, each filled with wicked rows of two-inch-long razor-sharp teeth. I could see why this species of shark was feared by many as a man eater.

Until that day, I had always felt that some of the shark stories told in the islands were but tall tales, to be taken with a large grain of salt. There seemed to be few verified shark attacks, and on the rare occasions when we spotted them while diving or swimming, they gave us no trouble, usually choosing to swim off after only the most cursory of looks.

Out of curiosity, Fletch suggested we open the stomach of our fourteen footer and I saw no reason why he should not.

"Go ahead, slit him open and let's see what he had for dinner yesterday."

Fletch smiled as he ran his big fish knife up the tough underbelly of the fish exposing the stomach sack. He then cut this open allowing two large bones and some smaller ones to fall to the deck. The stench was appalling, but it was the bones that took our breath away. The largest was one-and-a-half feet long and perhaps an inch-and-a-half thick. We looked at the deck in horror, as they were suspiciously human in origin. Although we hadn't heard any reports of missing persons, there were fishermen aplenty in the islands who fished from small skiffs, and whose disappearance could go unnoticed.

"Get rid of it, Fletch," I told him and without further urging, he picked the remains from the deck and pitched them over the side. We immediately gave the area an extra thorough scrubbing down with the deck buckets and powdered soap.

From that day forward, I viewed the shark with a new respect and if one appeared while we were swimming or snorkelling, I would call our group from the water immediately.

"Cooky," as Fletch referred to him, was Esau Mack, an Antiguan who had spent his life on schooners. Esau loved fish and made the best fish chowder I ever tasted. He was a cheerful man with white flecks in his dense black hair and eyebrows. His jaw was full of large white teeth, some of which had been gold capped. Esau had sailed on quite a few vessels over the years and had been to most of the islands of the Caribbean a number of times. He was quite a seaman in his own right and whenever we called all hands to make sail, Esau would appear on deck in his dirty apron and could be counted on to know the difference between the peak jig and the boomtackle. He was a real asset to the ship, but he unfortunately had three vices common to sailormen: rum, women, and gambling.

ESAU ISN'T HOLDING THAT TURKEY, SO WE MUST HAVE BEEN AT ANCHOR.

Esau was a well-known character in the Windward Isles, perhaps too well-known. Wherever the *Caribee* made port, there were always one or two local ladies on the dock asking for him, with little ones by their sides. Poor Esau would hide below and instruct the crew to tell them he was not aboard. Inevitably though, he would have to make the required trip to the local market to buy some provisions, and as soon as he stepped on the dock, the women would pounce on him and demand money.

Esau liked the rum as well and was particularly partial to the strong white mixture "Jack Iron," an unlabelled brew that kicked like a mule. And then there was the gambling. Esau was a compulsive gambler, never stopping until he exhausted all lines of credit. It was to be his undoing some years later. With all his faults, old Esau was a good-natured man and he knew how to cook.

The West Indian crew loved to fish and it was customary for them to cast a line from the bow when the schooner anchored for the night. The glow from the anchor light attracted schools of small fish, which swam in circles under the vessel. The deckhands sat and yarned, while pulling up a fish now and then. The fish were passed down through the galley hatch to Esau, who would clean them and add them to the fish stew he was preparing in a large pot on the stove.

ANCHORED IN HAVANA, CUBA.
LOU IS SMILING IN ANTICIPA-
TION OF SOME COCONUT ICE-
CREAM ASHORE AT THE CLUB

LOU, JANEEN, AND PETER
ARE THE *CARIBEE*'S
DECKHANDS-IN-TRAINING.

On one of these evenings, Esau was having more than a regular pull from the bottle of Jack Iron he kept hidden behind the spice rack. The crew were catching a nice selection of small red snapper and grunts, which they passed down to Esau on a regular basis. As time went on, the water level in the pot rose and wonderful aromas began to waft through the galley chimney and along the deck.

At dinnertime, I walked into the galley to see what delights Esau was cooking, and immediately became suspicious, as the unmistakably sweet smell of rum became evident. Any question regarding the sobriety of our cook was quickly settled as I looked into the large pot on the stove. There, amongst the onions and tomatoes, were a number of live grunt fish swimming around in circles. Under the influence of the rum, Esau had been putting the fish live into the pot. Talk about fresh! The fish stew was cancelled that night, but old Esau went on to prepare many more great ones.

The *Caribee* regularly sailed to Havana, Cuba where our guests explored the old city and rode the jitney buses to the rugged interior of this, the largest of the islands.

Once, while the *Caribee* was anchored off the Royal Club Nautico in Havana, Ernest Hemingway came in on his fishing cruiser, *Pilar*. It had been our habit for some days to go ashore to the bar at the club for a cocktail in the evening. We would take little Lou with us, who even at the tender age of five, was considered a regular. He and the bar man had established a strong friendship based on the sweet coconut ice-cream they made. Little Lou would sit at the bar and scoop up his ice-cream, while further down we downed our rum.

That evening, Ernest Hemingway walked in with Ava Gardner on his arm and I bought him a round. We talked of the sea and of the great fish that swam the blue waters around Cuba. Ava Gardner sat next to Lou and ate coconut ice-cream with him.

"He's really cute," she said and gave him a kiss.

Lou has always regretted not being twenty years older that evening.

We visited the massive citadel, built by King Henry Christophe in Haiti on the island Hispanola. He was the first black ruler of this island nation, and in fear of a French invasion, he built a massive fortress on the top of the mountain overlooking Cape Haitian. It is said that in the twenty years it took to build, thousands died hauling the huge blocks up the mountainside. King Christophe was so paranoid about security, he had the architects put to death upon the completion of their work. It is indeed one of the wonders of the world. It remains today a silent stone sentinel atop a Haitian mountain, a testament to tyranny and fear.

These were the islands of the great trade winds, which blew reliably from the north eastern quadrant for most of the year and our schooner revelled in the fresh breezes and warm tropical air. Our passengers drank sweet water coconuts in St. Vincent and hunted for mountain pigeon in Grenada. We visited the last survivors of the Carib Indians living in the mountains of Dominica. They, whose warlike ancestors once ruled the Eastern Caribbean, were now few in number, a vanquished but still proud people.

Terry and the children sailed with me whenever possible and Melvina would baby sit, while Terry handled the business. She was a wonder, my wife, always on top of the situation and nothing ever seemed to faze her. In September 1956, Terry returned briefly to Nova Scotia to see her parents, where she gave birth to our third son, Brian. She flew this time and was in good health when she returned to Miami.

In spring 1957, we sailed the *Caribee* on a voyage to Europe. It was a seven-month odyssey and more than fifteen thousand miles of blue water would pass beneath our keel before we returned. Our passengers were for the most part college students and they joined as amateur crew, sailing and working the schooner. It was a grand adventure and we sailed to Bermuda, the Azores, Gibraltar, Barcelona, Sardinia, Corsica, Greece, and Turkey.

LITTLE PETER WAS STILL IN DIAPERS, BUT HE WAS ALREADY
A TRANSATLANTIC VETERAN.

Heading westward in the fall of that year we suffered a violent storm in the Gulf of Lyon. The Mediterranean is famous for its short steep sea conditions, and this storm was no exception. We shortened down to storm trysail, reefed foresail and jumbo, and the cold northerly wind rose until it was blowing a full gale. We were on the starboard tack and the sea built until it was running at well over twenty feet and thoroughly confused as well.

Our schooner raised her stout bulwarks to windward, meeting each breaking sea as it hurled itself towards us. They would hit the three-inch thick apitong planks with a solid thump, and, breaking into a maelstrom of white spray, fly over the schooner.

Fletch and I stood cold and wet on the poop deck in our oilskins, as the stinging spray whipped across the deck. The two of us steered for those long hours as it took both of us to hold her. But, the *Caribee* was a fine sea vessel and we fought our way through without having to heave to.

From the North African port of Tangier, our group took a bus inland and we rode Bedouin camels in the shadow of the Atlas Mountains. They were temperamental beasts, and despite the efforts of my Arab guide, my mount seemed determined to throw, bite, or spit at me. I was relieved when our six-hour tour ended and I was able to regain the comparative safety of the bus. I suffered an awful pain in the back for days afterwards, a result no doubt of my camel ride.

Rounding Cape Spartel a few day later, we set squaresails on a southerly course. We paused briefly in the Canary and Cape Verde islands for provisions and water before the *Caribee* spread her wings once again for the long passage across the great Atlantic.

Terry schooled the kids from a correspondence course booklet she had acquired before our departure, but the children reaped a greater lesson in the day-to-day adventures of a life at sea. The *Caribee*'s tall spars returned to Miami in January 1958, and we took her to the Merrill Stevens Shipyard for a well deserved refit before starting our winter cruises in the Caribbean islands.

We began to spend more and more time further south and finally we ended up in Antigua in the Leeward Islands. Melvina went back to Jamaica, lonely for her family and friends and we missed her.

I suppose without really knowing it, I was searching for a base for my schooner, near to the area where we would be cruising, and also a place where Terry could settle for awhile and raise our young family.

English Harbour, Antigua, was the port where Admiral Nelson based his fleet in the West Indies. It is a landlocked harbour offering good shelter in most weather conditions and an excellent base for sailing vessels. This was the early days of the charter industry and there was only a half dozen or so permanent vessels in the fleet. A retired Royal Navy fellow by the name of Commander V.E.B. Nicholson kept his seventy-foot schooner *Mollyhawk* there, and they were struggling, as I was, to set up a permanent base for their charter business. Many a young sailing man made his apprenticeship from this port. Some, like Jol Byerly, Tim Hickman, Hans Hoff, and Joel Dressel sailed with me. They went on to become four of the most respected and knowledgeable skippers in the business.

It was in Antigua that Terry presented me with our fifth miracle, a tiny red-faced baby girl. We called her Michelle.

In time, however, I left the Nicholsons' in English Harbour, and explored areas further to the south. I finally found the perfect place in the idyllic lagoons of Marigot Bay, St. Lucia.

The Caribbean Sea

I HAD FIRST VISITED ST. LUCIA in the *Dubloon* and the images of Marigot Bay's landlocked lagoons were indelibly etched upon my mind. Halfway down the chain of mountainous islands, known as the Windwards, this beautiful isle offered some of the best anchorages in the Eastern Caribbean. Twenty-eight miles long by fourteen wide, St. Lucia's rugged coastline was punctuated by numerous white sandy coves and bays, where lush green ravines rose inland to the mountainous interior. At the southwest end of the island, the volcanic Pitons rose majestically from the blue Caribbean, serving as seafarers' landmarks since time immemorial. Marigot Bay lay halfway down the western coast, a pristine blue lagoon, unspoiled by man.

Years ago, the British and the French had fought bitter battles for this small island and it changed hands no less than fourteen times, but the island was still under British Colonial rule in the early 1960s.

During the years of World War Two, the United States maintained two bases here, Reduit Naval Air Station to the north, and Bean Field, a bomber base at Vieux Fort, near the south end of the island. PBY Catalinas flew from Reduit, while B24s patrolled from Bean Field.

St. Lucia sported what some called the world's only drive-in volcano, at Soufriere near the Pitons. This group of bubbling sulphur craters boiled and burst in grate spouts of molten mud and you could drive a car right up to them.

Marigot Bay was a place of breathtaking beauty, the kind of paradise one usually only dreams about. After a number of visits, Terry and I were so taken we decided to settle here and raise our children. Marigot was unique, with an almost magical aura about it, and so with the *Caribee* sitting serenely in her new anchorage we explored the land.

MARIGOT BAY AS IT APPEARED IN LATER YEARS. THE INNER LAGOON
IS AN EXCELLENT HURRICANE HOLE.

The bay consisted of two lagoons, an inner and an outer one, both as pristine as when they were first created. Lined with mangrove roots and sandy beaches, the shoreline sloped steeply inland with groves of coconut and other dense jungle. Fruit trees were bountiful: mango, plum, banana, and a score of others. The outer lagoon opened westward to the blue Caribbean and a short sandy spit of land covered in tall coconut trees semi-divided the two.

There was coral reef on the northern and southern edges of the bay, clearly visible through the crystal clear water. There was a good twenty feet of depth right to the head of the innermost lagoon, more than enough to float a schooner of deep draft. The inner bay was also totally surrounded by high mountains, which would bode well in a tropical hurricane.

The land was so green, we had never seen such dense green vegetation. The ground was pocked with huge holes in which the land crabs lived, those delicious foot-wide creatures we learned to trap and eat.

The evenings were a special time. Sitting on the *Caribee*'s stern, Terry and I watched the sun set at the mouth of the bay. We tried to catch the fabled green flash, which occurred just as the sun's fiery orb sank beneath the blue Caribbean.

The nights were enchanting too. Myriads of fireflies lit the dark, and through the night the loud chirping of tree frogs emanated from around the bay, keeping us company.

The tiny village of Marigot sat at the head of the valley stretching east from the bay, and was populated by the families of island fishermen who worked the coastal waters in their dugout canoes. They were a friendly self-sufficient group, most of whom spoke a dialect called patois, which we could not begin to understand. The fishermen wove beautiful fish traps from bamboo strips and used the bamboo sections as floating markers as well.

The island was a veritable Garden of Eden. Food hung from the trees in its season and the sea provided for those who had a mind to fish.

I investigated the possibility of purchasing some land, and eventually found Toby Wren, an old man who owned much of the property surrounding Marigot. In 1959, we bought some forty acres on the south side of the inner lagoon, and built our first home on it. A small three-room cottage; it was rudimentary, but would serve its purpose until we could fashion a more permanent home.

The charter business was evolving, and as the months passed by, Terry and I found the *Caribee*'s cabins were full most of the time. We also learned, however, that the clientele of the day were looking for more onboard creature comforts than our *Caribee* was able to offer, so we began our search for another, more luxurious yacht.

In the summer of 1960, we heard about the schooner *Gwenivere*, sitting in Oyster Bay, New York. She had just been listed for sale and I sent Terry to look at her. She flew up and after spending the day inspecting the vessel at the owner's dock she called me.

"She's beautiful Walter, just what we need," she said, sounding extremely impressed.

The owner, Mrs. Edith Montgomery, was an elderly lady who kept the vessel under cover for all but two weeks of the year. There was a huge boathouse and spar shed, where the masts and booms were housed when the schooner was not in commission. She kept a crew employed full-time and they spent much of the year varnishing and maintaining the yacht, so that it was always in perfect shape. During the fortnight of her birthday, Mrs. Montgomery would order her captain to commission the schooner for a few days of yachting, after which the *Gwenivere* would be put away again. Mrs. Montgomery was getting on in years, and after convincing her to part with the yacht for a reasonable price, we bought her.

THIS HERESHOFF SCHOONER EASILY SHOWED
THE *GERTRUDE L. THEBAUD* HER STERN. I OFTEN WONDERED
WHAT SHE MIGHT HAVE DONE AGAINST THE GREAT *BLUENOSE*.

She was a lovely steel Hereshoff vessel with glossy black topsides and expansive teak decks. From the tip of her bowsprit to the end of her main boom she measured 138 feet, with a beam of 24 feet. Her draft was fourteen-and-a-half. She had very luxurious accommodation for up to eight guests in private cabins aft, and an elegant walnut panelled wardroom, with a large gimballed table and plush seating. She was Marconi rigged and her wooden spruce mainmast towered 140 feet above the water. To port and starboard there were varnished mahogany motor launches for use when the schooner was at anchor. She was a magnificent yacht and I couldn't wait to put her into commission.

The *Gwenivere* had an interesting history. With a reputation as a very fast sailer, she was the only vessel other than the famous *Bluenose* to thrash the Gloucester racing schooner *Gertrude L. Thebaud*. Sailing under a different name, she met the new *Thebaud* off Gloucester under the able command of Ben Pine. Pine spoiled for a fight and *Gwenivere* obliged, quickly showing the Gloucesterman her stern. Captain Pine complained of a lack of wind and asked for a rematch the following morning. The *Gwenivere* once again obliged, this time in stiff breezes, but the *Thebaud* was sent home again following another sound thrashing.

If I have given the impression that I was a wealthy man, I should point out that these vessels were perhaps the last of the yachts of World War One vintage, and were priced affordably for people like me. The *Gwenivere* had been built in 1916 at the Hereshoff yard in Bristol, Rhode Island. Many of the vessels of this era had been commandeered during World War Two and used in the coastal patrol service. After the conflict, these wonderful old sailing yachts were often available for a pittance.

We decided to change the *Gwenivere*'s name to *Le Voyageur*, and in November 1960, we set sail, bound for St. Lucia with a delivery crew of ten, along with Terry and the kids. I wanted the whole family to enjoy our maiden voyage in this fine schooner, and we flew en masse to join Terry in Oyster Bay. Our first passage was a sea trial of sorts and the schooner proved extremely fast under sail, reeling off fifteen knots at times.

We stopped in Bimini for a day, where I picked up a few baby turtles from a local fisherman and gave them to the kids, who settled them in a pair of small plastic tubs in their cabins. Our next port was Miami, Florida, where we would load up with supplies, before setting sail for St. Lucia again. A funny incident occurred upon our arrival there. I called the kids together in the wardroom.

"Listen carefully now," I said in my fatherly tone. "If the custom's man finds out that you have turtles aboard, he'll take them away from you, understand?"

"Yes Daddy," they replied in unison nodding their heads.

As we approached our old anchorage off Bay Front Park, the custom's launch came alongside and the officer boarded the *Le Voyageur* to check our documents and clear us into the United States. I was completely surprised by what happened when the officer descended the main companionway to the wardroom, where we would conduct our business. For there, lined up at the foot of the stairs were my children, all standing to attention. As the officer came to the last step, their little voices chirped together.

"Sir, we don't have any turtles aboard, not even a one."

It was a classic moment and brought a smile to my face. The officer smiled broadly as well. He was good natured and let any suspicions pass.

"Well, just so long as you're sure," he said winking at them.

And so, the *Le Voyageur* came to St. Lucia and became the most successful schooner in the charter fleet. We painted her hull gloss white, which was much better in tropical climes. I hired a young seaman named Joel Dressel, who served as first mate, and with a total crew of eleven, we sailed on charter cruises from the Bahamas to the coast of South America. It was a fascinating life and our hard work paid off; we were a success.

I was later able to sell the *Caribee* to Twentieth Century Fox. They needed a swift looking Baltimore Clipper type for the movie, *A High Wind in Jamaica*, and *Caribee* was perfect for them. Later, when I took my children to see the movie, every time the *Caribee* appeared on the screen, they jumped up and shouted, "That's my boat, that's my boat!"

I was sad to see her go. She and I had been through a lot together. From the days of the vagrants of Bay Front Park to the great storm in the Gulf of Lyon, she had seen me through safe and sound. Fletch returned to Nassau, as he missed his people, and old Esau took some vacation and went home to Antigua. He was to join us again on the new schooner, but we never saw him again. I learned he was killed in a gambling fight shortly after he went home. He was a good man and we would miss his hearty laugh aboard the new schooner.

The following year, Terry and I decided to build a small hotel in Marigot Bay. I had secured the financial backing of a couple of partners, and we felt that with the increased yachting in the Windward Islands, there would be good trade for a bar and restaurant, along with a few rooms. We would call it the Yacht Haven Hotel.

We began work right away, hiring a gang of machete-wielding islanders to clear the brush. They were wary, as there lurked in the dense undergrowth the dreaded Fer de Lance snake, a deadly relative of the cobra family. They had been brought to the island by the British to reduce the rat population, which ironically the British had brought with them on their ships anyway. The British later introduced the mongoose to eradicate the Fer de Lance when it became a nuisance, but the mongoose was far more partial to the colonial chicken population, and much to the distress of the British planters, took a heavy toll on them.

LE VOYAGEUR'S FAVOURITE SPOT WAS OFF THE SAND SPIT IN MARIGOT, WITH
STARBOARD ANCHOR DOWN AND BOWLINE TO THE COCONUT TREES.

LE VOYAGEUR'S WALNUT PANELLED WARDROOM WAS
ELEGANT AS WERE HER GRACIOUSLY ATTIRED GUESTS.

SIMON, THE GOOD *GADUER*, HAD A MAGICAL CURE FOR ALMOST ANYTHING.

The island folk culture was heavily steeped in superstitions going back many generations, and the St. Lucians were guided in their day-to-day life by a host of taboos. For instance, if one was unlucky enough to meet a coffin in the middle of the road at night, then one had to turn and face away from it until it returned from whence it came. Under no circumstances should one try to pass.

The night was a time of danger when *soocooyons* (vampires) and other bad *lespuit* (spirits) wandered the bush at will, searching for victims. There were special lockets and pouches the islanders wore for protection against these spirits, and offerings could be left at the foot of the *peay formajay* (magic tree) to appease various deities.

One of our first employees in the bay was a regal looking man, who was obviously held in high esteem by the local villagers. He had greyish, tightly curled hair and his black face was contrasted by a mouth full of snow white teeth, which he displayed frequently in a ready smile. His eyes had a magic sparkle and he answered to the name Simon Innocent. What we did not know at the time was that Simon was, in fact, a *gaduer* or witch doctor. He seemed to take an instant shine to my children and in some respect took them under his wing. There began a relationship between him and our family, based on mutual respect that would last for as long as he lived. Simon would, over the coming years, act as a liaison between our two very different cultures, and make our time in St. Lucia both richer and easier.

In due course, we found out that Simon was a good *gaduer*, as opposed to one who used his or her powers for evil purposes. It was not long before we were to enjoy the benefits of his power.

One day, my youngest son Brian stepped on a large rusty nail the carpenters had left sticking out of a board. They carried him to the wooden shed which served as our construction office, where Terry was busy with some paperwork. She immediately sent a message to me on the *Le Voyageur*, which was anchored in the inner bay, and I came running. Simon had arrived as well and was even then taking precautions against infection. I ignored Simon and picking up the phone, called a taxi to take Brian to the local La Croix Clinic for a tetanus shot.

Meanwhile, Simon was continuing his own efforts. He took the nail which Brian had stepped on (one of the workers had saved it for this express purpose), and cutting a lock of my son's hair, wrapped it around the nail and took it to the magic tree, which stood at the back of the property. After voicing some special words, he hammered the nail, with Brian's blond lock, into the tree.

"No pwoblem," he said beaming proudly, "everyting alright now."

Naturally, I was less than certain of this and we took Brian to the clinic anyway, where a large nurse gave the poor little fellow a big jab in the bum.

Over the coming weeks, the construction workers at the hotel site took note of Brian's almost magical lack of infection. He suffered no ill effects from the nail puncture whatsoever, and for them it was obvious who was responsible for his "cure." Everyone congratulated Simon on a job well done, and his professional status as a *gaduer* was no doubt elevated. I was less sure about this, after all, my son had just received a tetanus shot.

I was sceptical, until I received a call from the clinic a few days later. The English doctor who visited the clinic twice a week called to inquire about my son's health. When I told him that Brian was fine, the doctor replied.

"Oh jolly good, I'm glad to hear it. You see I was a bit worried because I just found out that the nurse gave your son the wrong shot. We've been out of tetanus vaccine for two weeks now. She gave him a typhoid shot by mistake."

One of the labourers working at the hotel was a man called Remi. He lived alone on the high hillside overlooking the bay and for unknown reasons seemed a social outcast. Remi was feared by the villagers, and when anything inexplicable happened of an untoward nature, it was usually blamed on Remi. He was a bad *gaduer*.

It was our second year in Marigot and on Christmas morning Remi appeared at my door bearing a gift. It was the local custom for the villagers to raise pigs for slaughter during the holiday season, and one of the island specialities was a form of highly spiced pork sausage called *booden noir* or black pudding. With a huge smile Remi presented me with a large example of this gastronomic delight and in return, I gave him a bottle of Mount Gay rum. Each of us seemed happy with our respective gifts.

Half an hour after consuming this delicacy, I was writhing on the floor in such agony I had not dreamed possible. The pain in my stomach was excruciating and I passed out a number of times. Terry, who luckily for me always seemed to be at her best in times of stress, took charge and called the mate, Joel, from the schooner. He had the crew launch the *Le Voyageur*'s speedboat and drove me to the hospital in Castries town at thirty knots. The hour's wait for a taxi and the further hour-long drive to town could well have proved fatal. Joel did not spare the horses, however, and he got me to town in less than twenty minutes. The doctors pumped me out and flushed me clean, and I survived.

We found out that Remi had been in an argument with one of the schooner's crew, and he had made two gift puddings to deliver Christmas Day. One was made using the traditional recipe, while the other had been filled with poison. He had failed to tag the bad one and apparently got the two mixed up, resulting in the argumentative deckhand enjoying the good pudding, while I swallowed the poisoned one. Remi was not in the least apologetic, claiming that this was, after all, an honest mistake. I was not of the same opinion and fired him as soon as I was able to stand.

After clearing the land, we began construction on the main building. We used the local stone found in abundance along the shore for the walls. They called it "blue bitch" and we hired fishermen in their gomier dugout canoes to collect and carry it to the bay. The local masons carefully cracked the rounded stone, building beautiful walls and pillars. The canoes also carried sand from coastal beaches to mix with the cement. Lumber and other materials arrived from abroad in the local trading schooners; greenheart for the roof beams from British Guyana and tiles from Martinique.

This pioneer construction was an enlightening experience. Everything was done the old fashioned way. We mixed cement by hand, and even the gravel was reduced from the larger stone using only hammers. Twelve months later, we had nearly finished the first phase and we set a date for the grand opening. The final decorating was underway and the furniture and kitchen equipment from the United States was being cleared through customs.

THE MURAL SHOWS THE BRITISH FLEET HIDING FROM THE FRENCH IN MARIGOT BAY.

I located a company in England called Battleship Productions. They made furniture from the salvaged teak of decommissioned British war ships, which I thought was a grand idea. What better furniture to have in the dining room than tables and chairs built from the decks of British warships? The tables and chairs arrived in due course and were very impressive pieces. Each table was fitted with a small brass plaque identifying the ship it had been built from. My favourite one, which became my regular table, was titled "from the teak of the decks of *HMS Ajax* and *Achilles*, Battle of the River Plate." I found a book that recounted this famous sea battle, and I later saw the movie one night in Castries town. When I returned that night, I sat alone at my table and imagined what had gone before.

An artist named Barbara Ann Byfield painted a mural of the legend of Marigot Bay at the end of the hotel lounge. It measured some twenty by ten feet and depicted the story of Sir Samuel Barrington, the British Admiral who hid his ships from the French in Marigot Bay, by mooring them inside the inner lagoon and tying palm fronds to the masts. There were some interesting little nuances added into the painting. All of the partners were shown standing on the decks of the ships and even Terry appeared in the mural, as the figurehead on the foremost frigate, adorned with her fashionable gold-rimmed sunglasses.

On a trip to the United States some months earlier, I bought two ship model kits, one of the *Cutty Sark* and one of the *USS Constitution*. Lou and Peter built them and when they were finished, they were mounted in the dining room. The theme of the hotel was, not surprisingly, nautical and the stone construction caused many to enquire whether it was built on the ruins of some old British military fort. Texaco built a large dock out into the bay, which was at that time the only refuelling facility for yachts in the area.

Terry was heavily involved in the hotel's business and dealt with all the paper-work and accounts. She was also responsible for training the chambermaids, and this particular job proved to be more of a problem than she could ever have im-agined. The hotel had a main building with dining room, bar, kitchen, office, and a terrace overlooking the bay. The accommodation consisted of eight double-unit thatched roof bungalows, scattered around the tropical gardens. One day, Terry took three of the maids-in-training and gave them each the job of servicing a room. Two of the young women finished within a half-hour, but the third was nowhere to be seen. After awhile, Terry went to the room where the young woman was working and was surprised by what she found. One of her instruc-tions had been to put new toilet paper on the roll, and she was literally doing just that. The poor young woman was kneeling down in front of the holder rolling the paper from the new roll onto the old as neatly as she could.

Our chef, Mr. Portland, joined us with an impressive array of recommenda-tions from a number of international hotels. Hypolyte took command as bartender, and he made the best banana daiquiris ever.

THE WHITE GRENADINE SAND PILES UP. OUR NEW BEACH HAD ORIGINALLY LOOKED JUST LIKE THE MANGROVE-LINED SHORE ACROSS THE BAY.

NESTLED AMONGST THE COCONUT TREES, YACHT HAVEN HOTEL WAS READY FOR OPENING NIGHT.

MY FIVE CHILDREN SIT IN FRONT OF THE DENSE JUNGLE WHERE THEY LIKED TO HIDE AND PLAY.

In the beginning, most of the inner lagoon was surrounded by mangrove trees, the ones with the spider leg-like roots growing down into the water. The only sandy beach was too small and a larger one would be needed for the hotel. So, we decided if there was not one there, we would make our own. The mangrove trees were cleared away with the cutlass and the roots taken up.

There were still a number of sailing cargo schooners running between the islands, and I hired two of them to carry sand from the Grenadines to Marigot Bay to make our beach. The sand of the Tobago Cays was of a beautiful pink-white hue and Terry wanted this fine coral sand on the beach. The schooners sailed down to the cays to the south and moored on the shores of Petit Rameau. It took days to load up and more days to unload in Marigot, but before too long we were strolling along soft coral sand in front of the hotel.

The long awaited day arrived and the grand opening took place. Politicians, businessmen, and other important guests were invited. Marigot Bay had never seen so many cocktail dresses or coats and ties. Hypolyte was inundated with orders for his trademark banana daiquiris and other exotic cocktails.

Leroy and his four-piece empty oil drum steel band was out of tune, but what they lacked in musical ability they made up for in enthusiasm, pinging away as loudly as they could. I thought it was an awful racket, but no one seemed to mind. It was, after all, opening night, and after that everything would be a breeze.

Portland stood at the barbeque pit and grilled up the steaks, and I skulked around the periphery in a starched white shirt, while Terry took care of everything. She was in her element, organizing and attending to every detail and making sure the evening went smoothly. Meanwhile, the kids were slightly awed by all the goings on and looked on from a safe position. The grand opening was a success and the Yacht Haven Hotel was officially open for business.

I still sailed my schooner on her cruises, leaving Terry in charge of running the hotel. She was really amazing, considering all she had to do — raise five wild children, manage the hotel, handle the paperwork for the charter business, keep the accounts up to date, and still be able to smile at me when I returned from my voyages. She was a remarkable woman and I often wondered if she quite knew what she was getting herself into when she married me.

The *Le Voyageur* was a fine yacht, but I was always on the lookout for others. I suppose I was like the married man with a wandering eye. If I had one great vice in life, it was my love of sailing ships. To me they were alive, each with their own personalities and traits, and I understood them. We always speak of them in the feminine, and that is how I saw and loved them.

My financial partner, Frank Jameson, lived in California. He was a yachting man and had raced on the schooner *Goodwill*, in the Transpac once. It was he who told me about the *Ramona*, another schooner he had seen for sale in San Diego. She was a fast vessel and for many years held the record for a one-day run, 348 miles in twenty-four hours. I learned from Frank that the schooner could be bought for a good price, and so I travelled up to see her.

As I walked down the marina dock, I saw her tall spars in the distance rising far above the others. My heart quickened and as I came alongside her, I knew she was something special. She was another version of the *Le Voyageur*, and another Hereshoff masterpiece. I fell in love with her the first moment I laid eyes on her. Her long glossy white hull ended in a beautiful spoon bow and an elegant counter stern. The painters had given her a gold cove stripe, which accented her lovely sheerline. She was gaff-rigged and I could see that her racing rig would drive her well. The main boom hung out fifteen feet past the end of her stern and her varnished bowsprit seemed to go on forever. She differed from the *Le Voyageur* in that she had a teak dog house aft, just in front of the helm, but in all other aspects she was very similar to my own schooner. On deck she carried a fast looking varnished "Higgins" runabout and a lapstrake longboat. I met with the broker and hired a surveyor to look her over for me, and after spending the day poking around every nook and cranny aboard, I went back to the hotel and slept fitfully. I could not afford her. I had no cash at all, every cent was tied up in my shares in the hotel and the *Le Voyageur*.

My dream of purchasing the *Ramona* would come to fruition sooner than I thought. Mr. Louis Benoit, owner of Almeden Vineyards in California, subsequently chartered the *Le Voyageur* for a two-week cruise in the Grenadines. He enjoyed it so much that he asked me if I would sell the schooner to him. So I was able to secure enough cash to buy the *Ramona*.

And so the love of my life changed again. I felt a little sad as the *Le Voyageur* sailed away with her new captain, but how could I know what the future held?

THE *RAMONA* DROPS ANCHOR OFF MARIGOT'S SAND SPIT
AFTER THE VOYAGE FROM SAN DIEGO.

I sailed the *Ramona* from San Diego through the Panama Canal and back to the island of St. Lucia. Joel stayed with me and I began to groom him to take over the schooner from time to time, leaving me to spend more time with my family. He was a reliable young man and an excellent seaman.

Within a few months, there came about the first of many interesting episodes that put our little hotel firmly on the map. Frank Jameson was a mover. He was one of those individuals who made things happen. He was well connected politically in the U.S., and a millionaire in his own right. As president of a company supplying the military with missiles, he often dealt with the top brass of the army, navy, and air force, as well as senators and congressmen. He liked to tell everyone about his little hotel in paradise and the schooner yacht that was kept moored there. He was a tall, well-built man with a booming voice and a kind heart. He never once visited the island without a present for each of the kids. We were very fond of him.

Frank began sending some of his sophisticated friends down to Marigot to stay at the hotel. Terry and I were not overly thrilled at this, because the Yacht Haven was not really set up as a luxury establishment. It was early days for tourism in St. Lucia and the infrastructure was still fairly primitive. Our phone worked only sporadically and we shut off the power from our generators at twelve o'clock every night. Although a route had been bulldozed to the bay from the main road, it was still unsurfaced, becoming muddy and impassible in heavy rains. All in all, not the kind of island getaway to send clients who were accustomed to the Ritz. Anyway, Frank persisted and would phone Terry to say that senator so and so and his wife would be arriving in two days time, and in three days, to expect General Peabody and his wife, and to please take good care of them.

On one particular evening, he called Terry and told her to have the *Ramona* ready and the hotel on "code red alert" because some very important guests would be arriving soon. He said he was really going to put Marigot Bay on the map this time. There would be a group of twenty or more senators, congressmen, admirals, generals and even Mendel Rivers, coming to Marigot. Also included in the group would be the chairman of the Joint Chiefs of Staff of the U.S. military. They were to begin arriving in Martinique by large military transport in two days time, from where they would fly to the smaller Vigie Airport in St. Lucia aboard smaller aircraft.

Frank asked Terry and me to organize a party for the VIPs. A special plane was coming from Texas, he explained, with two hundred pounds of premium steak and fresh produce. Leroy's empty oil drum band was to be on standby and we were asked to invite the entire St. Lucia government, as well as the British representatives, Lord and Lady Oxford. Frank wanted all the prominent people on the island there to meet the U.S. brass.

Terry and I went into emergency operations mode as "D-Day" approached. The hotel was spiffed and cleaned and Joel, who I had recently put in command of the *Ramona*, was put on standby. On the appointed day, the first of the military planes landed in Martinique and later that day the wives of the various officials began to arrive in Marigot Bay. Frank owned a Beechcraft Bonanza aircraft, which he sent down to help ferry them from Martinique to Vigie Airport. Apparently, the wives had been sent on ahead, as the husbands were delayed due to some important affairs of state.

The wives had no idea of what to expect. They were enthralled by the beauty of Marigot Bay and enjoyed themselves tremendously the first evening, sipping Hypolyte's banana daiquiris, while chatting to each other by the bar. Even Leroy's steel band was a hit.

By the next morning the wives were settled in, but none of the husbands had appeared. The military men were held up, I was informed, by developments in the Far East, but they would be coming soon. Meanwhile, the wives were getting restless and looking for something to do. There were lots of questions like, "Where is the golf course?" or "Where are the tennis courts?" and "Where would I find the beauty parlour?" Unfortunately, we were unable to supply any such amenities, and so the wives stayed at the bar and Hypolyte continued to dispense his daiquiris.

Another day passed and by the next morning, Terry and I were worried. The big party was scheduled for that evening, but there were no husbands around and the wives were demanding to know what was going on. I called Frank.

"Frank, when are these people of yours arriving? I've got Lord and Lady Oxford arriving tonight, along with half the island and there's a group of rather angry women here," I told him. "You better get those men down here fast."

"Don't worry Walter, I think we may have everything settled here." Frank assured me, "and general this and admiral that will arrive tomorrow afternoon with senator so and so."

"But Frank, the party is tonight. Lord and Lady Oxford are going to be highly offended if you and the others aren't here. The whole St. Lucia government is going to be here with fifty of the island's most important people. What do you want me to do?"

"You're going to have to postpone it for a few days," Frank said, and that was that. Terry and I went through the embarrassment of cancelling the soirée. Telling the politicians was bad enough, but the frost came on the windows at government house when Lord and Lady Oxford were informed. The following day I called Frank again.

"Frank, you'd better get some husbands down here because there's talk of divorce going on."

"No can do, Walter, another problem has arisen," Frank replied apologetically, "Maybe you can send them on a short cruise. The men aren't going to be finished for a few more days."

The ladies were delighted with the idea and they were shifted aboard the *Ramona*, which was ready to sail under Joel's command. I told them they were going for a cruise of the Grenadines, a beautiful area to the south of St. Lucia. So, with young Joel at the helm, the schooner sailed out of Marigot Bay with a cargo of congressmen's and admirals' wives aboard, and a crew of ten. It was wintertime and the trade winds were blowing strong from the north-northeast. As soon as the *Ramona* spread her wings, she disappeared quickly over the horizon, lee rail down.

As luck would have it, no sooner had her sails disappeared, the phone began ringing. It was Frank calling to say that everything was cleared up and the men would begin arriving tomorrow.

The whole fiasco started up again. Frank and his entourage of generals, admirals, senators, and congressmen arrived, and loved the bay. Hypolyte couldn't fill the glasses fast enough and the cardboard box he kept to throw empty booze bottles in was soon filled to the brim. The first night was a roaring success. They all joked about how great it was for them to be sitting at the bar, while their wives were off sailing on a schooner. The seemingly humorous aspect of this situation was, however, short lived.

The following morning, everyone congregated on the hotel terrace and Admiral Carney cross-examined me.

"Walter, let me see if I have this right. You've sent the *Ramona* down to the Grenadines with our wives, and she's a schooner capable of more than twelve knots." I nodded for him to continue. "Now, my pilot has a yacht of his own and he tells me that the *Ramona* could be back tomorrow if we radio them now. Would you please oblige?"

I knew I was in trouble now. Facing the military might of the United States I said, "Admiral Carney, I don't know where the *Ramona* is right now, nor can I contact her as we don't have ship-to-shore telephone here, and as far as coming back at twelve knots, well the wind is very contrary at the moment and it would be a slow and rough return trip at best."

I could see this news wasn't sitting too well with these admirals and politicians, and I swallowed as they quietly digested my words. The next man to speak was Mendel Rivers, a big man with long white hair and bushy eyebrows.

"Captain Boudreau, are you telling us that you've sent our wives off to some little islands, you're not sure where they are at the moment, and you have no way of contacting them to get them back?"

I straightened my back and replied "That is the situation, sir."

There was a bit of turmoil amongst the ranks then and the big shots quickly turned on Frank.

"Well Frank, what the hell are you going to do?" they said. "You got us into all this."

There was silence. Frank and I could do nothing, save to sit and rack our brains for a way to resolve the situation. Even the kids were fascinated by this scene and were perched on the edge of their chairs watching and waiting.

"I know what to do," a familiar voice suddenly chirped up and all eyes turned towards the speaker. It was Terry. With a slight bow and a sweeping gesture of the hand, Mendel Rivers turned to my wife.

"Ma'am, you have the floor," he offered in a deep voice.

Terry stood up in her flowered dress, and as if this were an everyday affair, addressed the masters of the U.S. military.

"Well," she said smiling, "if you can't telephone them, why doesn't Walter fly down with the pilot of one of your fast airplanes and tell Joel to come back."

"But ma'am, how can he tell Joel if he can't radio from the plane?" one of the generals asked.

Unfazed, my ever-resourceful wife answered quickly. "That's easy. Just fill up a dozen or so of the empty rum bottles with notes and Walter can throw them out of the window when they find the *Ramona*."

There was another silence, followed by a few murmurs amongst our red-eyed top brass. Mendel Rivers lightened the tone by pointing out that after last night there would be no shortage of empty booze bottles. At that moment, I thought that any plan was a good one, and everyone else seemed impressed by Terry's idea. "Operation Rum Bottle" was activated immediately. I was never more proud of my wife.

The next morning Terry drove me to Vigie Airport and I climbed into the twin engined plane next to the pilot. She passed up the cardboard box full of rum bottles, all of which contained the same message; "Captain Joel, sailing yacht *Ramona*. Come home now, the men are in Marigot." Attached to each bottle was a long coloured streamer.

The pilot and I took off and flew quickly south. It was a fast plane and we were soon making a circuit of the Grenadines. Passing over the island of Bequia, I spotted *Ramona*'s tall masts.

"There she is," I said to the pilot and we got ready to drop our bombs.

"Just be careful not to hit the stabilizers when you throw the bottles out," he shouted to me.

I had always been wary of small aircraft and his warning left me feeling a little uncomfortable. I opened a window in the side of the cockpit and as we dive-bombed Bequia Harbour, I carefully threw out all the liquor bottles. We could see the local boys rowing out in their boats collecting the bottles.

We found out later that not only did Joel get the message many times over, the cheeky boys asked him to pay, charging anywhere from one to three of the local "Bee Wee" dollars per bottle. He stopped paying once he found out that all the bottles contained the same message.

Joel got underway soon afterwards and made the uncomfortable slog to windward under reduced canvas. It was squally and rough, with gusts to forty knots or more, but the schooner arrived the next morning and the wives were glad to get ashore. Some headed straight for their husbands to give them a kiss, while others headed straight to Hypolyte for one of his daiquiris.

The following evening, Frank Jameson finally had his party and even Lord and Lady Oxford managed the long drive to Marigot. Leroy and his empty oil drum band pinged away and the drinks flowed freely.

Mendel Rivers slept on the anchored *Ramona* for the balance of his visit and would drink a glass or two of rum while watching the sun set from the stern. Lou, Peter, Janeen, and little Brian sat and talked with him for a while one evening. They told him about the fish, the sea, and of the local characters who lived on the island. As they sat on the deck at his feet, he looked at my children from under those great bushy eyebrows of his and listened intently. Who knows what he saw in the eyes of these half wild young kids in the southern islands? Perhaps a trusting innocence, gone forever from his own way of life.

Later, during the winter of 1965, Admiral Carney chartered the *Ramona* for a two week cruise from Barbados to St. Croix. He came with his wife and six guests. I was in command at the time and Lou, Peter, and Janeen were at boarding school in Barbados. In fact, the three of them had just sailed up from St. Lucia with me and I deposited them at their respective schools before going to the airport to meet Admiral Carney.

We left Barbados at dusk with the intention of running down to St. Lucia, visiting the ports there and then proceeding north along the island chain, ending up at St. Croix in the U.S. Virgin Islands. I was wondering whether I would run into any problems with my guest, especially considering he was the first admiral I had ever sailed with. Unfortunately, things didn't get off to a very good start.

As soon as we left the lee of Barbados, the *Ramona* sunk her shoulder into the sizeable trade wind waves, running off at well over twelve knots. There was a good stiff breeze and the schooner was doing what she had been built to do.

Admiral Carney came to me after dinner and told me he would be retiring now and could he open the porthole over his bunk in the cabin, as he was finding it a touch stuffy. He was on the port side, which was the low side, and the *Ramona* was blazing along with her portholes mostly out of the water, but once in a while she would take a deep roll and put her midship ports under green water. The admiral was in the aft cabin, however, and I told him it would probably be alright, but that he should keep an eye out and close the porthole before he went to sleep.

Mrs. Carney was a very down to earth person, who didn't say anything unless it was worthwhile and I probably should have caught her eye when the admiral started looking for little favours. Anyway, just before midnight the wettest admiral you ever saw came up in his pyjamas.

"Do you have any idea what has happened?" he asked me in an angry tone.

I did in fact have a pretty good idea of what had happened, judging from his soggy pyjamas. But, before I could think of a reply he continued.

"Captain, my mattress is soaking, I am soaking. Why did you tell me to open the porthole?"

Since I was running my own vessel and not answerable to anyone, I was considering how to subdue the angry admiral, when Mrs. Carney came up the companionway dry as a bone and gave her husband a dirty look.

"Robert, you're a goddamn admiral, and if you don't have enough brains to close your own porthole, you can't blame it on the captain," she admonished.

We placated him by providing him with another mattress and clean dry sheets. I also had the steward close the porthole, of course.

Admiral Carney and I became good friends over the coming days. We would often sit in the dog house late into the night drinking coffee, laced with a drop or two of rum, and talk about the war. We remained in touch over the years.

The Voyage North

I CONTINUED TO SAIL THE *RAMONA* in the islands and she proved again and again she was a thoroughbred. We made some fine runs and the schooner showed us that she was capable of a solid fifteen knots, sometimes more. We organized friendly races, one charter yacht against the next. *Panda, Puritan, Harbinger,* and *Te Vega* were all fine large sailing vessels, but they would all have a good look at our stern as we left them in our wake. These were the beginnings of what would later become famous as the Antigua Race Week and the Grenada Race. The celebratory conclusion of the charter season, when we took part in gentlemen's races for a case of rum or a few cans of varnish; whatever we had on hand.

Returning from a charter one afternoon in late November 1966, Lou missed being badly injured by only a hair. We had been in the port of Castries for water and in the late afternoon we set sail for Marigot Bay, some six miles down the coast. It was a strange day and the wind seemed to be at a loss for which way to go. It was normal for there to be some funny wind in the lee of the island, but this day was different. The wind was waffling all over the place. The *Ramona* was under main, foresail, jib, and jumbo and was sailing just

THE *RAMONA* HELD THE
TRANSPAC RECORD FOR A
TWENTY-FOUR-HOUR RUN
FOR MANY YEARS.

THE WARDROOM WAS AIRY AND
WELL APPOINTED.

THE AFT STATEROOMS WERE
JUST LIKE HOME.

off Point La Toc. We were on the port tack and with the wind astern, the main boom was well out over the water. The boys were just getting the boom tackle ready to hook on when a freak gust came on from the west and the big sixty-five foot boom came crashing across the deck. The schooner jibed violently. I was standing just on the port quarter near the wheel when the boom came up short on the running backstays. The spruce spar broke into a mass of huge flying splinters. There were sharp jagged pieces of wood about ten feet long, flying around and I panicked momentarily as I looked for Lou, but could not see him anywhere on deck.

A short time later he appeared behind me, sopping wet.

"How the hell did you get soaked?" I asked surprised.

"Well, I saw one of those big splinters flying towards my belly, Dad, so, I dove overboard."

In the midst of the chaos, I had not even seen him dive, but I was glad he did. The longboat was towing astern and he had caught hold of it, climbed in and pulled his way back to the deck. I was still at the wheel and we lowered away the main. Luckily there was no other damage to the schooner and we had the shipwrights in Castries adze up a new spar within a week.

I was proud of my sons, as even at their young ages, they were as strong as grown men and excellent seamen. I dreamed someday of them sailing my schooner, but they were still attending school, albeit reluctantly. They spent every waking moment of their school holidays aboard and I hired their young St. Lucian friend, Lewis, as messman. He was a good lad and worked hard.

Joel served as mate for me, and when I needed a break, he would skipper the vessel between the islands. He was turning out to be a most competent skipper and would someday become one of the best sailing shipmasters in the islands.

Following a charter cruise to the Grenadines, we discovered that the battery in the Higgins launch had gone flat. The *Ramona* lay anchored in Marigot, with the launch along the starboard side. The speedboat was fitted with a big 240 hp V8 inboard engine and I called a gasoline mechanic from Castries to come and check it out. His was known by the nickname "Fordy," perhaps because he claimed to be an expert on Ford cars. He came aboard the schooner and we showed him to the launch. After only a few moments he rendered his expert opinion.

"De battery dead, skip. Jus have to give she a lil' jump start," he stated with authority.

We provided a long set of heavy-duty jumper cables and Fordy took over. Running one end of the cables through the hull porthole to the main engine-starting batteries in the engine room, he passed the other end down into the launch bobbing gently alongside. I climbed down into the boat to help Fordy, and he talked as he went about hooking up the cables.

"Positive to positive. Wait, no dat ain' right, it have to be positive to negative. Wait, lemme tink a minute," he said while scratching his head.

He finally hooked the black alligator clip to the negative battery pole, and before going to the engine throttle control, he handed me the positive end.

"When ah tell you push, skip, you push de end to de positive pole, right?"

"Right," I replied, rather uncertain about the rig.

Fordy rapidly worked the throttle back and forth, supposedly bringing gas to the carburettors.

"Yeah skip, touch it now," he ordered me.

The sparks flew as I touched the cable to the battery terminal, but the engine of the Higgins remained silent. Instead, I heard another noise. From beneath the schooner's counter came the deep muffled "flumph," "flumph," of the *Ramona*'s main engine as it roared into life.

Fordy was totally perplexed. "Eh eh? How dis could happen? Mussee a reverse polarity, skip."

He was all for trying again, but I declined his offer and we managed to have the speedboat's battery recharged at a gas station in Castries town. Fordy returned ashore to work on his Ford cars, where I hoped he would have better luck.

Our bosun was a shipwright from Bequia called Evan Hazel. He was a religious man who spent his off-periods reading from his Bible. Joseph, the second mate, was a St. Lucian and longtime employee of mine. The balance of the crew was made up of a cross-section of nationalities, but all were seasoned sailors and knew their work well.

One evening, while anchored at Pigeon Island, there was a heated discussion in the fo'c'sle. Hazel was berating the rest of the crew for their bad habits and warning of retribution from on high. He held his Bible in his right hand and pointed at whomever he was attacking at the time.

"All you bastards is jus' sinnuhs and back slyduhs," he accused everyone.

"Shut you mout', Hazel, you an' your bible makin' me vex you know," Joseph warned him.

"All you, you goin' to pay, de Lord goin' to strike you dung, jus' wait." Hazel ranted on.

"Hazel, you never run woman, eh," Joseph said winding him up a bit more.

Hazel became enraged then, raving incoherently while waving his Bible around his clenched fist.

"All you is bad men; you drink rum, you run woman, you gamble and you take de Lord's name in vain. Well, he goin' strike you dung, wait an' see."

It was a squally night and the gusts of wind blew through the cut between Pigeon Island and the mainland with a viciousness that surprised me. I ordered another shackle of chain out in case she had a mind to drag. There was rain, with thunder and lightening as well. At the height of the fo'c'sle argument, an incredibly loud blast, like a cannon shot, shook the schooner as a bolt of lightening hit the main topmast, knocking the brass cap off. It landed with a heavy thud on the deck a second later. As I came up the hatch, most of the crew were already on deck looking at the brass cap laying there smouldering by the main skylight. As we stood there in the stinging rain, there was a heavy smell of ozone in the air. No serious damage was done to the schooner, but we all felt a bit shook up, myself included. However, Hazel had seen the light.

"All you bastards, you see what you cause, de Lord send litnin' to strike you dung, you is evil men an' you all go dead."

Young Lewis was especially bothered. Anything to do with supernatural behaviour was dangerous stuff and he was of the opinion that following the lightning bolt, there was a good chance of a sword-wielding avenging angel descending to the deck to deal with the sinners.

Hazel packed his bags and signed off the following day. He was not about to put to sea with a bunch of evil men, whose chances of being "struck dung" were high. There was a noticeable decrease in bad language for a few days and the late night card games in the fo'c'sle ceased.

The *Ramona* was busy with the island cruises and we were making money, but I had special plans for her. She was rigged as a traditional gaff schooner and set eight working sails. She had a very big mainsail requiring many hands to work. I wanted to turn her into a three-masted schooner, thereby reducing the size of the main and making the whole rig easier to handle. I also wanted to put bulwarks on the vessel, so I contacted shipyards in Lunenburg, Nova Scotia, which I knew would be equipped to handle this rebuilding, and the plans were set in motion.

In late May 1967, the *Ramona* set sail from the island of St. Lucia bound for Lunenburg, Nova Scotia. I was in command, with Joel serving as mate, and we had a crew of ten to sail her. Lou, Janeen, Peter, and Brian sailed with me. Terry and Michelle would fly north and meet us in Lunenburg. Lou's young St. Lucian friend, Lewis, would sail as messman, and Oldrun from Roseau would be the cook. The crew called him "Oildrum," because he always used too much oil in his cooking. Joseph, who was the regular mate under Joel, was the bosun for the trip. There were a number of West Indian deckhands, including Rosemond Harold and "Acrobat" Jules. Peter Burke, another AB from Miami. Also, Christian Berg from Falmouth, Mass. Although Lou and Pete were still young, they would sail as deckhands on this voyage and were assigned watches as part of the crew.

Janeen helped when and where she could and Brian, who showed a keen interest in money from an early age, was appointed honorary purser. He had quite a collection of coinage from various ports and he kept these in a variety of locations for security.

Brian also held the part-time position of "bed warmer." The *Ramona* was not heated and the beds became cold when the regular occupants were on watch. Brian, like many young children, generated a lot of heat while sleeping and was paid by various crew members to sleep in their vacant bunks and keep them warm. He charged a quarter for each bed and he added this to his growing supply of coinage. Brian would, on occasion, take all of his treasure to the dining room table after dinner and count it out carefully, noting some figures on a little scrap of paper using a pencil stub. The crew gave him the nickname "small change," which did not seem to bother him.

After the ship had been provisioned in preparation for our departure, I called Brian to the dining room table and gave him a ten-foot-long grocery receipt, with hundreds of items on it.

"Brian, you have to add all this up and let me know if they got it right," I instructed him.

Little Brian took this very seriously and he diligently sat there for hours struggling with his problem. Of course, it was in jest, but Brian did not know this and after a couple of hours, we found him at the table crying his eyes out.

"I can't add it up, I can't add it up," he sobbed rubbing his eyes.

We all felt that maybe it had been a bit of a hard joke on Brian and as a sign of repentance, I gave him a crisp new American dollar bill, which seemed to reduce his misery in good measure.

The *Ramona* sailed north from the Windward Islands into the Leewards, stopping briefly at Antigua and Anguilla, before spreading her wings again for the Virgin Islands. The next afternoon we anchored in San Juan, Puerto Rico, where we stopped to buy an engine part.

When the launch was in the water, it would usually spend the night at the end of the boat boom. This wooden spar could be set at right angles to the hull and it served the purpose of keeping the launch from banging on the topsides. It was rigged with a tackle to haul the launch out to its end. There was a light at the end of the boat boom. Sometimes at night, huge fish would wait motionless under the bow of the launch waiting for the right moment to rush out and grab one of the smaller fish that were circling under the light.

While anchored off the Club Nautico in San Juan one evening, the crew were watching two really big fellows under the launch, and two or three more circling around waiting for the chance to take up this desirable position. Every few moments there was a terrific splash as one of them rushed out and took one of the school of fat mullet swimming under the light. Lou, Peter, and Lewis got their lines and hooks and tried every bait they had, but the fish were not in the least bit interested. Finally, Lou appeared with his rubber-powered speargun and after getting aboard the launch, he loaded it and laid over the bow. Those big fish were about five feet long and six inches across at the head, and we still didn't know what they were. As the largest one slowly poked its head out of the shadow of the launch, Lou let him have it right square in the top of the head. Well, I never saw such a fuss. The huge silversided fish jumped and splashed all over the place, almost pulling Lou into the harbour. He held onto the tether cord of the spear though. There was a lot of thrashing around and yells of "Pull the boat in" and "Don't let him get away," but the meter-long spear shaft was well and truly lodged in his head and Lou wasn't about to let him go. We pulled it in and Lewis put the gaff into its back, swinging it onto the deck of the schooner. I hadn't seen a fish like it before, but Peter Burke was able to identify it.

"That's the biggest snook I ever saw," he said astonished. "I didn't know they came that big."

When we weighed him on the scales, he tipped in at over sixty-five pounds. He tasted pretty good too when we fried him up the next day.

Continuing our voyage, we passed through the Sargasso Sea, northeast of the Bahamas. There were miles of brownish coloured seaweed, which held an amazing variety of sea life. I recounted to the kids the mysterious tales of ships trapped for eternity in the brown weed and of old men with long white beards, captives forever in the Bermuda Triangle. But for us there was no danger and we had great fun gaffing clumps of the seaweed and laying it on the deck. The kids made their own seaquariums, filling buckets with seawater and then shaking out the seaweed to find whatever was in it. Brian was especially fascinated by this, spending hours examining the tiny creatures as they fell out of the weed. He picked out the little shrimp, crabs, and sargassom fish, along with dozens of other tiny species, and put them in his bucket.

Just southwest of Bermuda, we were caught in a blow and had to heave to for twenty-four hours. The *Ramona* was on the port tack and we struck all sail, save for the jumbo and the storm trysail. She was heeled over rail down with only these two pieces of sail. I think that this was the first time Lou, Peter, Janeen, and Brian had really experienced a storm at sea. For them, however, it was still an adventure. They were totally trusting in me, a feeling of confidence, which was complete. In their eyes, I could sail them anywhere and through any storm. I took this trust seriously.

While the wind howled overhead, the kids spent hours looking down into the depths of the sea through the hull portholes, which were continuously under water. It was a greenish-blue world and they kept watch for any fish or other sign of life down there, but none ever appeared. The ship rolled over onto her beam ends whenever she was hit by an especially vicious gust, and she would sink her lee rail a foot or two below the sea. The waves came steadily from the windward side and made heavy thumping noises on the hull, as driven by the wind they hit the *Ramona*'s bilge. It sounded like a huge hammer was striking the ship and we felt her shiver every time. But old Nat Hereshoff had known his business, and the riveted steel plates held fast. There was water coming in from above, however, as the hatches leaked when the occasional big sea came aboard.

The Higgins launch sat in large teak chocks on the deck. Even though she was lashed down well, she struggled to break loose whenever a big sea came aboard. The wire straps holding her to the deck were strong though, and they held.

Even though the helm was lashed, each watch was required to report on deck to keep an eye on the storm trysail and jumbo, in case either one showed any sign of parting a seam or ripping. We stood lookout, making sure there were no other ships near to us and checked the bilges half hourly to make sure there was not any water coming into the vessel.

It was a time of tension on the schooner. I allowed Peter and Lou on deck only under my protection, taking them by the shoulder to the dog house where I told them in no uncertain terms to stay put. They watched the storm from behind the windows and huddled in their jackets from the wind. Each big sea rose ominously in the distance, and then, building momentum, they would crest and break just to windward of the schooner. It always seemed as if those towering seas would come crashing aboard, but most of the white frothy maelstroms would rush violently towards the schooner only to roll harmlessly under the keel. Occasionally, an exceptionally large wave crashed over the rail and washed the decks. The *Ramona* was flush-decked, however, with no bulwarks and the water would disappear over the lee rail almost as fast as it came aboard. Every once in a while, though, we witnessed immense waves a long ways off from the schooner. Their foamy white crests looked ominous as they rose high above the rest of the sea.

Throughout history the mariner has feared the rogue wave and we were no exception. It has been surmised that occasionally the long ocean swells rolling westward across the great Atlantic Ocean will form into rogue waves as they hit the eastern most limits of the Gulf Stream as it winds its way north. I cannot say for sure, but the wave we experienced that day must have been one of these.

I saw it first and it took me a moment to realize what it was. Towards mid-afternoon a thin grey line had appeared on the horizon to the east and initially I thought that it must be an approaching squall of some sort. But after a few seconds, I realized that this could not be, for whatever it was, it was approaching from leeward. I took the binoculars and what I saw caused me to shiver inside my pea jacket. A white foaming crest lay almost unbroken across the horizon for at least two miles, and I could see the sea spume as it was blown backwards from the tops of the jagged crest. How could this be? I had seen all manner of ocean swell and wave, but this defied all common sense. It was a monster wave of impossible proportions.

I called Joel and we made what preparations we could. The wheel was double lashed and all hatches checked to make sure they were secured from within. I took my children to the aft cabin and quickly threw a handful of cushions to them in the hopes that this would help. There was little more I could do for them and I felt that I should be available near the deck to take some action, should it become necessary. I thought about striking sail, but decided against this as the schooner would roll uncontrollably. As sailing men know, it is always best to keep

sail on in bad weather, reducing in increments. I stood with Joel in the main companionway where there were two low ports from which we could see out.

The giant wave took only a few minutes to reach us. I felt a terror grip
my guts as the wall of dark grey water rose beside the schooner. We lost
sight of the sky, and all of a sudden the wind ceased to blow. I watched in
horror as the *Ramona* was thrown upwards like a match stick until her
bowsprit was pointing into the sky. I heard the pots and pans and all manner of cutlery flying around as the schooner was held almost perpendicu-
lar. Shouts of fear and terror came from the wardroom, as furniture and
fixtures broke loose and fell upon the crew, as they themselves were thrown
to the bulkhead wall like flies.

I held the mahogany rail with a vise-like grip, as for one terrifying moment
I thought the ship would fall backwards into the ocean. The ports suddenly
went dark as the ocean overcame our vessel, and I felt the schooner shudder
as if being shaken by a giant hand. The wave had fallen on us and the *Ramona*
was for the most part submerged at that moment. The cold sea water came in
through the cracks in the hatches and the main wardroom glass skylights burst
inwards, allowing a rush of water to invade the ship.

And then it had passed. Our schooner shook herself again like an animal
emerging from the water, and as she rose to the surface she freed herself of the
tons of water which had covered her. The wind returned in a vicious gust and
she heeled over once again. The jumbo was gone, only a few shreds of tattered
dacron remained on the forestay. The storm trysail had miraculously survived,
but the heavy sheet tackle had parted like thread and the sail was flogging thun-
derously. We called all hands and after attending to the trysail, began to square
away the ship. Save for a few cuts and bruises, no one was badly injured. The
engineer had started the pumps and the water that had flooded the bilges was
soon sent back to its place of origin.

The *Ramona*'s interior was a mess and everything was wet. Lou and the others had come to no harm in the aft cabin, but I was amazed by their comment.

"Oh gee Daddy what a fun wave, can we do it again?" they asked cheerfully.

It was the innocence of youth, but I was happy enough. We had survived a
rogue wave of immense proportions. Joel and I later guessed the height at no
less than sixty-five feet.

The balance of the bad weather seemed decidedly benign and the crew returned to the deck to stand their watches, even though the wheel was lashed.
Going forward with Joel and two men, we bent on the old spare jumbo and
after an hour had the schooner hove to under sail again. The storm blew itself

out during the night and in the morning, I ordered sail on and the *Ramona* continued on her way, battered but proud.

We stopped in Moorehead City in the Carolinas to effect a clean up and enjoy a day or two of rest. It was here that we had first hand experience with the foulness of racial discrimination. It was a nasty surprise for the West Indian crew members. My children had grown up with the black people of the islands and they had certain ideas on how the different races fitted together on this earth. Brian had once asked Terry one day why our skins were a different colour.

"Why, they just spend more time in the sun, that's all," she replied. It was an innocent enough explanation and possibly not far from the truth, as sunlight affects pigmentation.

My children grew up knowing that the island people were culturally different, but that they were equal as well. They went to church and so did we. They ate, slept, and drank the same way as us. If they cut themselves, they bled the same red blood. They knew sadness and joy and expressed these feelings in the same ways.

The crew had some shore leave coming and those that were free got ready to hit the Carolina town. There was a John Wayne film on at that time called *War Wagon* and Joel took Lou, Peter, and Lewis. It was only a short walk from the yacht. They lined up to get the tickets and Lou began to notice they were getting some odd looks. When Joel reached the counter to buy four tickets, the lady in the booth said, "No N____ allowed in here."

It was a terrible situation, and as Lewis walked away from the cinema, Lou told me later on, he glanced back with a very hurt look on his face.

Lou later asked me about this kind of discrimination, but for once I had no sensible answer. How could I explain this other than to say it was wrong? From that moment, the friendship between Lou and Lewis changed. No longer were they the special friends who had sailed and fished together for so many years without racial animosity. There was now a hidden wall, and even though they remained friends, they both knew that something had come between them. Whenever they spoke, there was a slightly guarded feeling that they were not being totally open with each other, and there was somehow an inequity in their lives.

During our stop in Moorehead City, I had the strangest encounter. A small forty-foot sloop with a blue hull was moored just ahead of us on the dock and she flew the German flag. Her solitary skipper was a slim, balding fellow with a short white beard. I was standing on the dock near the *Ramona*'s bow one evening when he came towards me. He walked with an erectness that spoke of some military history. He introduced himself and we spoke for a time about ships and the sea. And then we broached a subject that both of us had experienced first-hand, the war of the North Atlantic.

"I was captain of a submarine before I was captured," he told me in a German accent.

"You were captured?" I asked.

"Yes, I only made one cruise to the eastern coast of America and then my submarine was sunk by a destroyer, but most of my crew survived."

Out of curiosity I asked him the number of his submarine and I felt an odd shiver at his reply.

"It was *415*. You know it?"

"Nineteen-forty-three, remember the old square rigger north of Bermuda? That was me."

He looked straight at me, and as a cloud shadow passed overheard, a frown crossed his face.

"I remember. I am sorry, it was war."

"Yes, it was war," I replied. I could not think of anything else to say.

"I must go now, goodbye."

As he walked down the dock he turned to look towards me once more. "I am glad you lived," he said to me. It was a profound, honest gesture and I took it as that.

He returned to his vessel and I went back aboard the *Ramona*. My crew was still working on some small rigging chore and in an attempt to divert my thoughts I needlessly busied myself with them, saying nothing of what had just passed. Later, after the day's work was finished, I sat on the fo'c'sle hatch to enjoy a pipe of good Borkum Riff tobacco and a glass of Mount Gay rum. Just before sunset, the small blue sloop left its berth ahead of us and moved slowly into the channel. As I watched her disappear, I reflected inwardly, trying to fathom my feelings towards the German captain. I thought that I should have felt hatred or, at the very least, anger for had he not left us to perish on the open sea? It was indeed strange but I experienced no animosity at all. Perhaps I should have felt forgiveness, or even gratitude that they did not machine-gun us as we sat helpless in the lifeboat, because, God knows, there was a lot of that going on.

I took a deep pull on my pipe and closed my eyes. I was taken back to the days in the lifeboat and the *Angelus*; to my shipmates, the topsail yard arm, and the tattered red ensign at the peak or the main gaff; to our brave Captain Jensen and his little dog, Mutty. Oddly enough, I felt the hint of a smile pull at my lips.

Despite the cruel awfulness of the end, there had been good: A tall ship, fine men, and some happy times. I knew then that there could be no forgiveness, just the reluctant acceptance of a trial long past. Too many have used the word "war" as an excuse, numbing the human conscience. I felt a sadness for those who had been lost, but no anger for the man who was even now sailing his little sloop into the Atlantic. He would have demons aplenty to accompany him on his solitary way and, in any case, my anger had been used up all those years ago.

As I went below to sleep, the chance meeting seemed to fade into nothingness and I wondered yet again if it had really taken place. That night I dreamt of an old square-rigger with patched grey sails on a calm sea. By dawn the next morning the faces and events surrounding the *Angelus* had become, once again, just a memory.

The *Ramona* sailed on and made her way north within the Gulf Stream. We prepared some bottles to cast adrift with messages. Janeen, Peter, and Lou all wrote notes asking that, "Whoever finds this note, please reply to the schooner *Ramona*" and listed our address. Lou received a reply to his note almost a year later from a boy in Norway, who had picked up the bottle on the shore there. Later, Janeen got a response from a lifeguard in Virginia Beach. She felt that even though her bottle had not travelled quite as far as Lou's, it didn't matter because the lifeguard was most likely very handsome.

The Gulf Stream is the sea river north, and as long as we stayed in its warm flow we would enjoy as much as sixty to ninety free miles a day. The sea was a vibrant indigo blue here, while overhead puffy white tradewind clouds sailed across the powder blue sky. There was always a small sea running, but under her canvas our schooner remained steady, moving only gently beneath our feet. I felt content; my fine schooner sailing well, my children with me, and mother ocean seeing us along our way.

The sea life was abundant. Every day, swarms of birds hovered over schools of fish and we saw bigger ones breaking water as they chased their prey. The schools of flying fish were endless, darting along like little shiny missiles from wave top to wave top. Whales blew from time to time near the schooner and the porpoises played under our bow like wayward children out from school.

There were two or three days in the Gulf Stream when the fishing was probably as good as any I will ever see. As the *Ramona* sailed northwards, the two trolling lines were hardly ever without a fish on the end and we caught tuna, wahoo, and dolphin. There was a pile of dolphin and wahoo on the foredeck that never seemed to decrease. These were the green-gold coloured dolphin of

AS WE SAILED NORTHWARDS ON THE *RAMONA*, THE FISHING WAS
THE BEST WE HAD EVER KNOWN.

the fish family and not the "Flipper" version. They were also known as dorado in the islands and were a great-tasting fish. Young Lewis was there with his fillet knife and as fast as he filleted out one pile of fish, a dozen more were swung aboard.

I climbed up the ratlines on the main mast until I was forty feet off the deck. From that vantage point, I could see far out over the blue Gulf Stream, and I saw the flashes of green and gold as the dolphin made passes at the feather baits astern. I watched two or three being caught while up on my perch. They struck viciously at the bait and as soon as they were hooked, they flew into the air, making a terrific show on the surface. We caught two large bluefin tuna one day, which went deep on the lines and we had a hard job getting them to the surface. When we finally hoisted them aboard with the fish gaff and put them on the scales, they each weighed in at just over a hundred pounds. We caught a few small sharks, one of them a sixty-pound pointy nosed mako with jagged teeth. He never stopped jumping until he was alongside the vessel.

Eventually, I had to tell the crew to roll in the lines and stow them away as the freezers were full. There were a lot of hungry mouths on board, though, and luckily everyone loved fish.

As we passed the northern limits of the Gulf Stream, I felt a pensive mood come over me. It was calm with just enough wind to keep the *Ramona* going and we were due to come onto the southernmost edges of George's Bank later that day. We set topsails after breakfast and the schooner was under full sail. I spent part of the day sitting on the foredeck hatch looking out to the northeast thinking of a time long past. I had passed this way before. That evening, as the stars sparkled, Lou and Peter joined me. I smoked my pipe and told them of an old square rigger called the *Angelus*, which I had sailed on so many years before and the friends that I had lost. Who knows? Perhaps their ghosts still wander the wave crests to the east of George's Bank, guiding mariners who pass their way.

We were becalmed on George's Bank the next day and the schooner sat like a toy on a mirror-like sea under a grey sky. We watched as big shark fins slowly cruised along the surface, and after awhile Joseph pointed out a really big one and we all got up to have a look. This dorsal fin was at least three feet above the surface and the tail followed about fifteen feet behind. It appeared as if the fish was going to pass very close by and Peter Burke unlashed the big harpoon from the foremast shrouds. This was a swordfish harpoon, with a detachable dart and a ten-foot wooden handle. It was attached to a five-gallon float by a length of good stout line. Burke was a big strong fellow with a muscle builder's physique and he got ready with this weapon at the rail. This was not a normal activity on the schooner, but I agreed to let him have a try. The shark swam sinuously along the surface towards the *Ramona*. When it looked as if it was going to swim by on the port side the crew lined the rail.

Unbeknownst to me or anyone else, Lou had grabbed his rubber-powered spear gun and was leaning out from the main rigging between the turnbuckles, aiming it at the shark. The big monster came cruising right alongside the schooner, no more than eight or ten feet away. Burke hauled back and let fly with the harpoon, but missed completely. The shark turned sideways then and his big black eye seemed to look straight up. Suddenly, Lou leaned out as far as he could and fired his little speargun at its head. But he also lost his grip and fell in. Well, the story goes that Lou walked on water that day because he hardly got wet. His legs were in the water up to his thighs before he knew it, but he managed to catch hold of a turnbuckle with one hand. He scrambled back on deck with such speed, he even surprised himself.

"Just what the hell were you trying to do?" I boomed at him angrily.

Lou was so shaken he could not effect an answer. He sat on the hatch running his hands up and down his legs, thankful he still had them. The rest of the crew, however, were having a tremendous laugh at his expense, and they didn't let him forget it for the rest of that trip. Peter later told me that he had seen the shark make a sudden move towards the splash that Lou's legs had made, but it had not followed through.

As we sat drifting, the boys put lines over and caught codfish for dinner. That afternoon a fishing trawler showed up and gave us our position. We were almost where we thought we were. The fishing vessel came close alongside and they threw a large halibut to our deck, which I filleted for the fridge.

On the day of our arrival on the coast of Nova Scotia, we were greeted by a dense fog. The radio had forecasted it, but they didn't say how bad. The West Indian crew had never seen fog before and when Lewis came up on deck that day, he ran around stooped over, his eyes squinting. I heard him talking to Lou.

"Smoke, where all dis smoke comin' from?" he asked.

"It's fog," Lou told him authoritatively. I found this rather amusing, as Lou himself had never seen it before either.

"What you talkin' frog, dis is smoke, man," Lewis replied emphatically.

We closed the coast, but the fog never lifted. It was a thick soup and I could not see the bow of the vessel from the stern. There had been no sun to take a sextant sight for two days now and I was running on dead reckoning. The wind died away completely, leaving the sea calm and still as glass. We lowered away all sail and started up the machinery. The only sound then was the muffled belching of the main engine as it pushed us slowly along.

For me, it was a homecoming of sorts. I had left this cold north country in 1951 and my children had never seen it through adult eyes. Lou had been a baby on the *Dubloon*, and now some sixteen years later, he was returning to see the place of his birth for the first time. Lou and Peter were teenagers now and I was proud of them. They were doing men's work on a deep-sea schooner and I showed them no preference over the rest of the crew. I was keen for them to see the coast of Nova Scotia, where their roots lay.

I began to feel a bit anxious when I realized that we had run down our distance and still had not sighted land. I estimated we should be near our destination of Lunenburg, but there was no sign of it, only the dense fog. We had three lookouts, one aloft in the foremast crosstrees and one on each side of the bow.

After a time, we heard the deep forlorn drone of a fog horn and we reduced speed, leaving us coasting through the water. Joseph stood by with the lead line to take soundings. We tried to hone in on the signal because Joel and I felt it was a buoy and not a ship. Eventually, we the saw the steel marker emerge from the fog just ahead of the schooner. We quickly launched the longboat and Lewis and Lou rowed over with a bowline from the schooner and made it fast.

"Not exactly legal," I said to Joel, "but under the circumstances we'll do it."

We swung to the buoy while Joel, Joseph, and I looked on the chart. The number indicated that we were tied up to the Pennant Cove marker, just south of Halifax. The current had taken us north much faster than I had calculated and we had overshot our destination by a fair margin.

It wasn't long before a pretty-looking lobster boat appeared out of the fog. It was Melvin Grey and Charlie Maryatt, returning from their days fishing.

"Ahoy," they shouted waving at us.

"Ahoy back," I replied as their boat came alongside.

"Where you from?" they asked putting a hand out to fend off.

"We're from the West Indies bound for Lunenburg," I replied.

Animated smiles crossed the fishermen's faces.

"You don't have any of that good island rum aboard by any chance, do you?" one of them asked laughing.

"Ever tried Mount Gay rum?"

"No, never heard tell of it, good stuff is it?" the man at the helm asked.

"The best. But, right now we need a safe place to anchor until the fog lifts," I said.

"Oh, well now you just cast off there and follow me in, and I'll just put Charlie here aboard to stand on the bow," Melvin said.

And there followed an amazing feat of seamanship. Melvin's lobster boat took up station ahead of the *Ramona*'s bowsprit and after casting off we followed slowly. The fishing boat drifted in and out of the fog like a ghost, while Charlie stood on the bow relaying directions aft.

"Come to port just a little."

"That's it now, starboard two spokes."

"Steady as she goes now, hold her just like that."

We could see nothing as I steered the *Ramona* through the thick fog, but after awhile the sounds of the sea breaking on rocks could be heard.

"Sounding," I called forward.

Joseph started to swing the lead line and when he had a good arc, he let the lead fly forward. It splashed in the water thirty feet ahead of where he stood at the base of the forward rigging.

"By the mark five." he called back to me.

"By the mark five."

"And a half four."

After about twenty-five minutes our ghostly pilot slowed to an idle.

"Get your anchor ready now," the word came back, and then "Stand by, you can stop now," and "Go slow astern."

All was quiet on the schooner's deck. We didn't know where we were and still could see nothing. There was a difference now though. The surface of the sea was truly calm, the type of flat calm found only in sheltered water. The ocean had ceased to roll and the *Ramona* sat solidly in the water, her decks moving not at all.

"Let her go now," Melvin shouted from his craft, and after a signal from me, Joseph swung the hammer at the pin holding the big fisherman anchor on the davit. With a loud splash it plunged into the water.

The chain rattled out, stopping after a shackle and a half. We looked around but there was still nothing to be seen, just the quiet stillness of the water and the blanket of fog. There was a mystical aura about, an earthy smell, and I caught the scent of pine trees and salt cod, but for all of that there was no indication that we were anchored anywhere other than on the high seas.

The lobster boat came alongside again and Melvin Grey climbed aboard.

"How do you think we're laying?" I asked.

He peered into the thick fog for a moment before answering in a confident tone. "Good enough, you give her a bit more chain and she'll be just fine."

The schooner's crew and the fishermen then turned to more important business and I sent Lewis down into the hold to bring up a case of the "good island rum." I called the crew into the wardroom and everyone took a large glass of the golden liquid. Truth be told, we all ended up having more than a glass or two, and in the evening, the fishermen went ashore for their wives and children, who came aboard to join the party. They brought two large fat salmon back, which I traded for a few bottles of rum, both parties being well satisfied.

It is no secret that Nova Scotian seamen have a reputation for being very partial to this golden elixir, and we were no exception. We drank and sang and then drank some more. It has been said that the heaven to which Nova Scotian seamen aspire to go to at the end of their days is located in the St. Pierre and Miquelon rum warehouses, where reside more barrels of strong rum than perhaps anywhere else on earth. It must have been a stroke of good luck indeed for a big schooner with a few cases of rum in her bilges to make landfall in Pennant Cove.

Late in the evening the party ended, and the fishermen climbed back into their lobster boats, along with their wives and children and went ashore, all with an extra bottle or two under their arms.

As a crisp clear dawn broke the following morning, I experienced a moment of panic. We were anchored well into tiny Pennant Cove. To seaward lay a small channel with jagged rocks on either side. Ahead of us stood the fishing village and astern an islet or promontory with pine trees. It was indeed a daunting feeling to look at the opening through which we had come, and to realize we had done so blind. The Pennant men, with the knowledge of a lifetime of fishing from their cove, had brought us in through the thickest fog without a problem. Even in good clear weather I would have thought twice about entering here.

Later that day, the customs man arrived to inspect the schooner and accept our manifests. He was a portly gentleman with a very serious expression on his face. I passed him a bottle of Mount Gay rum and all of a sudden he didn't have much interest in looking over the vessel, and he returned to the shore in a most jovial mood, after wishing us "*bon voyage.*"

A day later we made the short passage to Lunenburg and all hands were on deck as the schooner made harbour. The crew quietly prepared the mooring lines and as we approached the docks of the Lunenburg Foundry, Lou and Peter perched themselves in the foremast rigging. The engine room telegraph jangled and the heaving lines were thrown. We came alongside the dock and the long voyage north was over.

Mader's Brook

WE ALL HAVE DREAMS AND I HAD ONE for the *Ramona*. It was to turn her into a schooner better suited for my Caribbean charter business. To do this, I planned to make three basic changes. First, I would add a third mast, the mizzen, splitting her big main into more manageable sized sails. I had plans drawn up by a reputable naval architect so that it was engineered properly, but even more importantly, looked correct. This would make my ship no less swift, but would certainly make her easier to handle. Secondly, we would build waist-high bulwarks all around, making her safer and drier in a seaway. Thirdly, we would add two square yards on the foremast for downwind work. In addition, we planned to give her a new deck as well as refit all of her existing systems, putting her in tip-top condition.

I spoke at length with Jim Kinley of Lunenburg Foundry and Engineering and the work began on the *Ramona*. She was berthed alongside the Foundry docks and the workers began her transformation. They removed her spars and booms, and her old decks were ripped off exposing the steel frames. The chipping hammers nattered away and zinc chromate was applied to the bare steel. Soon the schooner began to look like a construction project. We stripped her of gear and equipment, which was either placed in storage or sent to the warehouse to be repaired or replaced. Sails went to the sailmaker's shop to be renewed or restitched. The engines were stripped and new parts ordered. Electricians began wiring and welders cut the steel for the new bulwarks, while the shipwrights milled teak for her new caprails.

Terry and I rented a small house in Mader's Brook, not far from Lunenburg, where we would spend the summer as the work progressed on the ship. The house was located at the head of a cove, just fifty feet from the shore. There was also a little wooden dock across the road.

Janeen, Brian, and Peter enrolled in the Lunenburg Yacht Club, where they were to enjoy the benefits of the summer sailing and swimming program. There was also a junior golfing program that the others joined, but Lou couldn't see the point of chasing a little ball around the meadow. In the beginning I was at a loss about what to do with him. With the shipyard work going on aboard the schooner, there was nothing for him there and he seemed slightly ill at ease with the other young people at the yacht club. He was a rather shy young fellow and the life he had led so far left him ill-equipped to interact with the North American youngsters of his own age. They knew nothing of "magis noir" or West Indian culture, and while the lads of his age at the club were learning to sail eighteen-foot centreboard sloops, Lou's hands had already been hardened by the sheets and tackles of a deep-sea schooner. My children had made many ocean voyages by this time and Lou was not about to have someone instruct him in the intricacies of sail.

Salvation came in the form of the *Ramona*'s longboat. I loaned it to him for the summer and he brought it around to Mader's Brook, mooring it just in front of the house. It was a twenty-two-foot wooden craft built especially for the schooner. She had a sailing hull and was also equipped with a nine horsepower Evinrude engine, which pushed it along at six or seven knots. It had oars and a mast with loose footed lugsail.

Lou outfitted the craft with fishing lines and a small compass from the yacht. I provided him with a chart of Mahone Bay, which Terry placed in a plastic chart holder to keep it dry. He had a small anchor and line in case he needed it. His last piece of equipment was the old faded straw hat that he had worn for so many years in the islands. It had a knotted cord, which he snugged under his chin on windy days.

On most mornings of the week, anyone who bothered to look out would see the tanbark lugsail of the longboat as it left the confines of Mader's Brook headed for the open sea. Occasionally, Peter would go with him, but mostly he would go alone. There were plenty of fish to be had along the shore in those days and Lou would always return with the wooden crates in the bottom of the longboat filled with fish; cod, pollock, haddock, and mackerel by the score. There was always fresh fish on the table at the little farmhouse in Mader's Brook.

We became friends with Jim Kinley, and Lou and Joel occasionally crewed on Jim's fine racing sloop *Gypsy* out of the Lunenburg Yacht Club. She was a beautiful craft and the Kinleys kept her in tip-top shape.

During the summer, there was the annual Lunenburg Fisheries Exhibition. There was a junior section in the dory races and I registered Lou and Lewis as dory partners for the two-man race. They practised every evening for a month before the race and we thought they were pretty fast.

On the day of the race, they took their dory to the starting line and got themselves ready. The coast guard cutter stretched a line out from the dock and the sterns of the dories backed up to it. There were eight dories and we waited in anticipation of the gun. When it was fired from the cutter, Lou and Lewis were first off the mark. They were rowing like hell, and having spent years rowing together in the islands, were pretty impressive. In the first few moments they took a strong lead. Terry and I stood proudly on the shore with excitement rising as they pulled. Lou was in the stroke position, that is, he was aft and Lewis was in the forward seat and had to mark time with Lou's strokes. They were going great guns when all of a sudden Lewis started laughing like crazy. His voice carried clearly to the shore.

"Man, we winnin,' we winnin,'" he cried excitedly.

His joy at being ahead caused him to break stroke and catch a huge crab, and they never recovered the winning rhythm. The two boys came in fourth out of eight, though, and Terry and I were pleased.

The *Ramona* gradually took on a new shape as the summer wore on. The new decks were laid and caulked and the new mizzen mast stepped. New wire rigging was spliced up in the loft and the big steel turnbuckles were sandblasted and re-galvanised. The foremast now had three square yards and a new bowsprit was installed. The bulwarks were built, raising the cap rail three feet all around the yacht and giving her a much different aspect on deck. She suddenly seemed a lot bigger. The teak deck houses and hatches were all refinished and given many coats of shiny new varnish. All her masts and spars were scraped down and revarnished and the new sails bent on.

I spent every moment of my time on the schooner during the refit. The anchors and chains that had been sent away for galvanizing came back, and the long inch-and-a-quarter stud link chain was drawn aboard and stowed. The boat davits were replaced and the boats fitted for new chocks.

At the end of the summer, Lou brought the longboat back around to Lunenburg and the shipyard crane lifted it onto the dock. The shipwrights made templates of the hull for the new chocks and she was settled on the deck and lashed down.

Terry and the children flew back to St. Lucia in September. She would see them off to their various schools and then begin preparation for the reopening of the hotel, which had been closed for the summer. Lou was especially reluctant to leave.

"I want to sail back to the islands," he grumbled.

But he was scheduled back at Mapps College in Barbados and I would not let him take the time off.

The long summer was at an end and the *Ramona* was not ready to sail. By November, I was faced with one of those conundrums that require one to make a difficult decision. I was needed at the hotel back in St. Lucia, where various construction projects were ongoing and needed to be finished before the start of the winter season. I really didn't have time to sail the ship south. Joel, who would help me sail the vessel in the islands was very competent, but did not have the necessary licensing to satisfy the insurance. There was no question about what I wanted to do—it was a question of what I had to do. So, after some consideration, I decided to look for a qualified master to take her south.

Not long after I put the word out, Captain MacKay was recommended to me and we met at a tavern in Lunenburg for a chat. I needed to come to a decision

THE *RAMONA* REFLECTS HER NEW RIG ON THE CALM WATERS OF LUNENBURG HARBOUR, A FEW DAYS BEFORE SHE SAILED FOR THE WEST INDIES.

quickly regarding this and I got the information I required right off the bat.

"Captain MacKay, do you have any doubts about your ability to handle the *Ramona* and take her south?" I asked him.

"I have no qualms whatsoever," he replied.

I checked his qualifications and made a few calls regarding his references, which were bona fide. He seemed to be a man of some considerable experience under sail and I was satisfied with his credentials. After discussing at length the many details over a number of days, we agreed on a delivery price and shook hands.

"Well captain," I said, "the *Ramona* will be ready to sail in a couple of weeks, so why don't you come down now and Joel will show you around her."

Joel took it all very well. He must have felt a little awkward in the sense that he was going to skipper the ship once it reached the islands. However, he placed himself at MacKay's disposal and acted accordingly.

My dream had come to fruition. I had transformed a Hereshoff schooner into a three master. As she sat there at the docks in Lunenburg, I felt such love and pride it threatened to burst from my chest. Her long sweeping bulwarks ran from bow to stern, topped with a fine heavy teak cap rail. The rig looked perfect, her three spars lined up just as I had envisioned so many months before.

She would see our family's charter business into the next decade for sure. She would be the queen of the West Indies charter fleet and none would challenge her.

On November 26, I watched Captain MacKay motor the *Ramona* slowly out of Lunenburg. A number of harbour craft escorted her out, and as they passed Battery Point the schooner set her jib and foresail. Even though it was cold, I stood on the Lunenburg Foundry docks and watched until her tall spars disappeared into the mist. There were ten crew aboard, including Dr. Ken MacIntyre, a young Lunenburg physician who signed on to make the trip south. There was Joel, Lou's friend Lewis, and six others.

I returned to St. Lucia immediately to help Terry open the hotel for the coming season, and on December 2, I was called to the phone at the office where I was given the heartbreaking news. Terry watched as my face turned white and my whole body began to shake. The *Ramona* had been wrecked on the reefs north of Bermuda, and there had been loss of life. Five of her crew had drowned.

Peril on the Sea

THE DISASTER HIT ME HARD. I thought of the men drowning in the surf and my lovely *Ramona* being pounded on the reef. A terrible nightmare had me drowning in a turbulent sea, and it left me weak and bathed in sweat. There was a sadness in our family now and it was a very difficult time. After calling the insurance company, Terry booked me a ticket to Bermuda and I flew north to attend the marine inquest and examine the possibilities of salvage.

I had, of course, been to Bermuda before and always enjoyed this colourful island, but now it seemed unfriendly and unforgiving. By the time Joel and I got out to the wreck, the *Ramona* had slipped off the coral ledge and was now laying in twenty-five feet of water, with only her three spars showing. A pair of divers went down to try and retrieve the logbook, but they did not find it. It was the strangest feeling to sit there in the motorboat and look down at the *Ramona*'s white topsides through the clear water. One part of me still wanted to believe that it was all a bad dream.

The investigation convened quickly, and I attended with the survivors. The court of inquiry ruled that "Captain MacKay was guilty of incompetence and misconduct, which resulted in the grounding of the barkentine yacht *Ramona* on Bermuda's North Rock Reef on December 2." His master's licence was cancelled. The *Ramona* was judged fully sound and seaworthy and no blame was placed on the owners.

After the insurance investigators spent a day on the wreck site, my ship was declared a total loss and any hopes of salvage were dashed. They decided that the total loss policy amount would be less than the cost of raising and rebuilding the ship. I had no option other than to accept this decision, as I could not raise the salvage costs on my own.

Over the coming weeks, I was able to piece together the events leading up to this tragedy. The *Ramona* had left Lunenburg under the command of Captain MacKay, a master mariner, with a good record of experience under sail. The voyage began well enough, the schooner excelled under her new rig, and Joel was pleased as he took her measure. The trouble began when they ran into a bad winter storm northeast of Bermuda. As seafarers know, the north Atlantic can raise great tempests and this was one of them. A huge sea built and the wind rose to sixty-five knots and more. The *Ramona* took a terrible pounding and blew some of her sails out. However, she was a good strong ship and she might well have survived this trial had the decision not been made to close Bermuda during the storm.

As Captain MacKay brought the *Ramona* closer to the island, she took the reefs near North Rock, some six miles off the island, and was washed into the coral beds, where huge breaking seas battered her hull. She would not sink at that time, as she was in only six feet of water, but she lay mortally injured on her side in the grip of the coral, while her crew huddled in the dog house.

Through the long hours of darkness, the wind howled and waves broke over the schooner again and again. Against Joel's wishes, Ken MacIntyre, young Lewis, and three of the other crew took the longboat and a dory to try and make the shore. They could see the lights of Bermuda shining, but they were deceptive. They appeared to be much closer at night than they really were, and it was these crew members who lost their lives as they fought to row ashore. They were caught in the strong surf and drowned. Those who stayed aboard

I COULD HARDLY BEAR TO LOOK, THERE HAD BEEN LOSS OF LIFE AND MY DREAMS WERE SHATTERED.

SHE WAS IN ONLY TWENTY-FIVE FEET OF WATER AND I HAD HOPES OF SALVAGE.

were saved. They held on through the night as the surf crashed over the vessel's hull, and in the morning the conditions eased enough for a boat to pick them up.

I felt terrible about the men who had lost their lives, and I tried to offer some solace to their respective families. It was not easy. I was the one who had to try and explain to distraught mothers that their sons would not be coming home. Terry, as always, was a pillar of support. She had gone through everything with me over the years; the good and the bad, but this was to be a hard mountain to climb.

Lou came home from school when he heard the news that his best friend had drowned, and this was difficult for him to accept. At sixteen he was learning what all seafarers must learn, that the great ocean can be a cruel mistress. I understood how he felt and sometimes I would watch him sitting on the dock in Marigot, looking expectantly out the harbour. Peter and Janeen understood what had happened, but Brian and Michelle were too young to fully appreciate what had taken place.

There were many details to attend to and I set about them like an automaton. Before leaving Bermuda, we laid Lewis and the others who perished to rest in the seaman's cemetery.

We settled with the insurance company, but the amount of the policy was below her real value and we took a financial loss as well. Some months later, a group of Bermudians headed by treasure hunter Teddy Tucker salvaged the *Ramona*, but when she was finally floated they found that her once proud hull was twisted beyond repair. It was a sad end to a fine ship.

Back in St. Lucia, I did what I could to help the families of those who had been lost. We built a small wooden cottage for Lewis's mother and I gave the others what monetary help I could.

A year or so later while visiting Bequia, I met up with Evan Hazel again. He was the Bible-pushing crew member who had warned the crew of retribution from on high following the lightning strike on our mast.

After hearing about the *Ramona*, he was quick to point out to me. "Dem fellas was punished by god for dere evil ways."

"That's crazy, Hazel, they were all good men," I replied angrily.

I believe those who go to the sea in sailing ships are a special breed of people. They seek something they cannot find ashore. A peace perhaps, or maybe that feeling you get when you stand on deck at night under a sky full of stars. But they will always know there is risk, and that from the earliest time, sailors have perished on the great sea.

STEPPING ABOARD THE *LE VOYAGEUR* I FELT AS THOUGH
I WAS BEING REUNITED WITH A LONG LOST FRIEND.

I steeled myself to carry on. I knew we had to try and put this behind us a soon as possible. We still had charters booked and if I could find another ship, well, we just might survive. We needed a lucky break and we got it. The schooner *Le Voyageur*, which we had sold to Louis Benoit earlier, came up for sale, and so after discussing it with Terry I flew down to Coco Solo in Panama to look over her. It was May 1968. I began to feel better the moment I saw her long white hull swinging gently to her anchor, and when I stepped aboard it was as if time had stood still and I had never sold her in the first place.

Mr. Benoit had sailed her out of San Diego for a few years and she had been a regular visitor in many of the yacht clubs on the west coast. He had enjoyed the yacht and had put a lot of money into her, but for personal reasons he had to give her up. She was then donated to the United States Naval Academy as a sail training ship, but they found her too big for their purposes and she was given back to Mr. Benoit. At this time, the *Le Voyageur* held little value to the wine grower and he was impatient to sell her. I made a good deal with him and the Boudreau family owned her for the second time.

She was laying at the U.S. naval base in Coco Solo, Panama and I took her over from there. Louis Benoit had made some improvements to her, including adding a second diesel engine, turning her into a twin screw vessel, but the propellers were of the feathering type, so when she was under sail they did not drag or slow her down at all.

Lou, Peter, and a number of others flew down to help sail her back to St. Lucia. Ian Cross, a young Canadian sailor whose family operated a seventy-five foot Alden schooner in the islands joined our crew, along with old Jed McCarthy, a friend of the family, Huboldt the steward, Jongue the seaman, Philip from the Canary Islands, and a few more. I met them at the airport and they could see I was a changed man.

Owning a schooner again was an elixir to me and I was told that my eyes once more held that special sparkle. How unpredictable life can be. The schooner I had once owned and sold was now mine again. I knew and loved the *Le Voyageur* and I had a sense that we belonged together.

We left Panama and sailed to Curacao, where we dry docked the schooner and painted her before laying a course for Venezuela, where we planned to fuel up at their low rates. The main seaport of La Guaira is located on the coast below the city of Caracas, which sits up in the mountains. The port is man-made, with two breakwaters. The entrance to the port is narrow, but would easily allow the passage of two good sized vessels at the same time.

We sailed into La Guaira and were directed by the Port Authority to a location in the inner mole, where we berthed the schooner alongside the dock. I let the crew take some shore leave, while the cook took advantage of the cheap provisions. Our fuel tanks were filled to brimming with cheap Venezuelan diesel, at a rate of only a few cents per gallon. After two days in port, I wanted to get going, and so we prepared the ship for departure the following day.

Early the next morning, I went to the office of El Capitano del Puerto, to get our clearance. He was a short pudgy little man with a pot belly and moustache. His uniform was flashy, with lots of gold braiding and he wore a shiny black holster on his hip with an oversized gun in it. He was a pompous fellow and as we stood in front of his desk he totally ignored us, pretending to look at some papers.

"Sir, we are leaving now and I would like to get our clearance," I said to him holding out my crew lists and ship's manifest.

The little "El Puerto" (as we secretly named him) looked up, rolled his bottom lip out and raised his head into the air, contemplating his reply. It was an almost comical Mussolini-esque affectation. After a moment he looked sideways at me and in the most condescending voice gave me the following verdict:

"Imm-possible, there are seex American warships coming to visit Venezuela today and the port is close-edd to all shipping, excep-ted those ships."

"What, so you mean we can't leave?" I asked incredulously.

"No, you must stay in your position until tomorrow, or maybe the next day. You must wait until the entrance is clear-edd," my inflated little friend said. He then waved his hand, dismissing me.

I thought to myself as I walked out the door, "I'll be damned if I'm going to sit here waiting for the U.S. fleet to come in," and as I walked back to the schooner, I hatched a little plan which would take care of our problem port captain. As soon as I crossed our gangplank, I gave orders to have everything ready to go at a moment's notice.

Around ten o'clock that morning, the first American destroyer appeared outside the breakwater and I gave the word to get underway. The engine room telegraph jangled and we backed slowly away from the dock. The destroyer was just making its approach to the breakwater entrance. At that moment little "El Puerto" came waddling down the dock with a number of *Guardia National,* machine guns in hand.

"Halto, stop, stop. Imm-possible, *el puerto cerrado!*" (the port is closed), he screamed in a high pitched voice. In his agitation, the words came out "esstop, esstop."

As the schooner's stern slowly swung away from the quay, I turned and held my hands out in a gesture of innocence. "No speekee Spanish. *Adios,*" I replied.

This really infuriated "El Puerto" and he had a fit right there on the dock, screaming and shouting while jumping up and down and waving his arms in the air. His face turned purple and he took his gold braided hat off and threw it on the ground.

I figured it was time to put more distance between us and I rang up three quarters ahead on the engine room telegraphs. Our bow swung quickly then and we headed for the entrance of the harbour, timing it so that we would pass the warship in mid channel. Although from a distance it seemed as though it might be a tight fit, there was easily enough room for both vessels. I lined up the schooner's bowsprit in the left hand side of the channel and on we went.

A moment later, a sleek looking, grey-painted Venezuelan patrol boat came roaring out from the Port Authority dock, headed straight for us. She was moving fast with a huge white bow wave and the irate "El Puerto" on the foredeck. Two *Guardia National* soldiers manned the machine gun mounted there.

We passed alongside the U.S. warship with room to spare. The American sailors were lining her decks at attention, the position they usually took for entering port. We also stood at attention and at the moment when we were closest, Peter dipped our large U.S. ensign to salute the ship. The warship gave us a toot on the horn and all their sailors saluted our ship as we passed. The officers on the bridge waved at us and the giant American flag at their stern dipped, acknowledging our salute. It is a maritime tradition that ships of the same flag salute one another. The Venezuelan patrol boat slowed down and swerved away. They had seen we had a big friend.

We laughed and talked about our little adventure throughout the day. It had been a cheeky plan, and although not one I would recommend, it had worked. It was probably not a wise move to antagonize the *Guardia National*, but I didn't appreciate being held prisoner by the harbour master, who was just trying to bully me and act superior.

That night, as we sailed slowly along the Venezuelan coast, a grey patrol boat came close alongside and shone powerful spotlights on us. Their crew were manning the big machine gun on the bow, aiming it straight at us. After awhile, however, they left us and went on their way. Perhaps it was "El Puerto" just letting us know that he had not forgotten our little trick.

We sailed on and the morning found us with a fine breeze, the schooner close hauled and making good knots to windward. We were on the port tack and the dense jungle of the South American coast lay some ten miles to our south. Towards noon, we came about and set the fisherman topsail to add another knot or two. With luck, we would fetch up under the lee of Grenada that night. Within an hour we had sunk the Venezuelan coast beneath the horizon astern of us and we were alone on an azure sea.

After a long conversation with Lou during that trip, it was agreed that he would not return to school. He wanted to become a sea captain. My only condition to this agreement was that he would not be allowed to hang around Marigot Bay. If his desire was to make a life on the sea, then that is where he should be. He left shortly thereafter to sail on the great schooner *Bluenose II* and follow his heart. He was not yet seventeen.

It was a time of new beginnings. Terry and I decided to rename the *Le Voyageur*. She would now be known as the *Janeen*, after our eldest daughter.

Islands to Windward

AND SO WE ENTERED A NEW ERA. Nineteen-seventy came and went in a blur and it seemed as though the years were flying by and I was a bystander watching the proceedings from a distance, but this was not so; we were in the midst of it all.

With Lou away at sea and the others still in school, Terry and I had a little time to ourselves. The Yacht Haven Hotel took up most of her time, the *Janeen* took up most of mine, so we were always busy. Months passed by and life was good again. Like a grave illness, the terrible blow that we had suffered began to recede slowly into the past.

I still followed the wind and sailed the islands of the Caribbean. The *Janeen* was very successful in the charter business and we were always booked throughout the winter season. We were lucky that over the years family members often came to help sail our vessels. They enjoyed the sailing and I put them to work on whatever jobs needed doing. My brother Bob and his wife Gloria made voyages with us as well as others, including my young niece Simone.

We had reached a balance in our lives and there was a stability now, where before there had been restlessness. Many people asked me if I ever tired of taking my schooner to sea. But how could I tire of that which sustained me? The *Janeen* and I had some wonderful adventures together and each day was a new page in the logbook of life.

We bought a piece of land on the bluff overlooking Marigot Bay and built our dream house. It was of an unusual design, open-sided to the west, and built of hard island stone and tropical woods.

In 1972, Lou and Peter came home from a voyage to Europe and sailed with me for awhile. It is a wonderful thing when a man can go to sea with his sons.

Our charter cruises often took us to the beautiful island of Dominica in the Windwards. Wild and primitive, her lush green mountains rose precipitously from the sea, while deep jagged ravines ran inland from bays and coves with black volcanic sand beaches. Of all the Windward Islands, Dominica, with its verdant jungle, was perhaps the most naturally stunning.

ALTHOUGH IT TOOK SOME YEARS TO COMPLETE, WE WERE HAPPY WITH OUR NEW HOME ON MARIGOT BAY.

The village of Portsmouth is situated at the north end of the island in Prince Rupert Bay, a large natural harbour giving superb shelter in most weather conditions. A long sandy beach lined with coconut trees ran from the colourfully painted houses and shops of the town to a heavily treed bluff to the north.

Nestled in the rugged mountains above the village, a lush green valley held the only remaining enclave of pure Carib Indians. At the time, these were perhaps the last living remnants of the once war-like tribe, who had ruled the islands of the Eastern Caribbean. A company called Dominica Safaris began operations that year using zebra stripped Land Rovers, with drivers dressed in bush jackets and safari hats. They drove tourists into the remote mountainous centre of the island to visit jungle waterfalls and old plantations, the high point being a visit to the Carib Indian reservation in the north.

The Jungle River runs inland from Portsmouth town and we often took our guests there in the launch to see the many species of exotic birds and dense tropical rain forest lining the banks.

In January 1973, while anchored in Portsmouth, we had the good fortune to see "Venus," a most remarkable woman. Lou and Peter were with me as we sounded our way into the northeast corner of the bay, just off the Spotlight Restaurant, which happened to be the only entertainment establishment there at the time.

Within a few minutes of the anchor hitting the bottom, a fleet of little row boats, manned by young local lads, came out to us with fresh fish, vegetables, straw hats, and various handcrafted pieces. Some offered coral jewellery and turtle shells, while others had conch and live lobsters. This floating carousel market circled around us, eager to sell their wares.

LOU (RIGHT) AND PETER TAKE A PULL ON THE *JANEEN'S* MAIN STAYSAIL
SHEET AS SHE MOTORSAILS ALONG.

One particular rowboat, slightly larger than the others, came alongside with a dark and distinguished looking gentleman sitting at the stern. He introduced himself as Mr. Lamb (he pronounced it "Lumb"), the owner and operator of the Spotlight Restaurant.

When he felt he had gained the attention of a few of our guests and crew, Mr. Lamb launched into a well-rehearsed and animated pitch.

"Come to de Spotlight Restaurant. We have everyting; steel band, limbo dance, Venus, de belly bottle dancer, and bahbeque mountain chicken," he said smiling and waving his arms.

He caught everyone's attention with the bit about Venus the belly bottle dancer, and we leaned further over the rail to find out more.

"What does this Venus dancer do then?" one of our passengers asked.

"Venus is de exclusive performer at de 'Spotlight' and de main ack is de bottle dance, " Mr. Lamb obliged.

We were all ears.

"She does de belly dance, de limbo dance, and den she does mash up all de empty bottles in de resraunt, an do de bottle dance pun de bruken glass," he finished emphatically.

This brought a few guffaws from guests and crew alike. It sounded as though Mr. Lamb was a con artist trying to lure clients into his restaurant.

"Doan laugh, what I say is true," he said in earnest.

The host of our charter party turned to me in amazement.

"You mean she dances on broken glass, Walter?"

"I guess. Do you want to go in and find out?" I replied just as curious as he was.

"I think we better go see this," our guest said, and so I booked seats ashore at the Spotlight restaurant for the show and barbeque dinner.

Generally during charter cruises, the crew was not allowed ashore, but I made an exception this time, so that Lou, Peter, myself, and a couple of others could witness this event. I was fairly sceptical about the impending entertainment and of the opinion that this was still some sort of gimmick to lure the tourists ashore. Still, everybody seemed game and so, while our guests prepared themselves, the crew gassed up the launch and cleaned it out in preparation for the evening's ferry service.

At seven o'clock, we made our run to the beach in front of the Spotlight. It was calm and we were able to put the bow well onto the shore, so that our guests could disembark without getting wet. Mr. Lamb had the area lit up with kerosene torches, plus a few electric lights in the restaurant itself, and the steel band was already pinging away. The Spotlight was right on the water's edge and built of woven coconut palm siding, with a thatched roof held up by bamboo poles. Tables and chairs of roughly sawed local cedar timber stood awkwardly in the sand, surrounding a twenty foot cement dance floor in the centre.

Our party was soon seated at the ringside tables, where they were served powerful rum punches with hibiscus flowers popping out of each glass. We were the only visitors, other than a few locals at the bamboo bar. The evening menu was delightfully simple. You could choose rum punch or Carib beer, and either mountain chicken with breadfruit, or mountain chicken with rice and vegetables. Our guests chose the rice version. Mr. Lamb then told us he had once visited America and been to a seafood restaurant where you could choose your own live lobster straight out of a tank. He was so impressed by this, that he installed his own program along the same lines.

"Yeah man, you can choose you own mountain chickens," he said proudly ushering our passengers towards the back.

We followed him behind the bar where, in a dimly lit corner, stood a grotty chicken wire cage inhabited by dozens of really huge frogs.

"Wait a minute, you said you were serving chicken?" I asked slightly taken aback.

"Yes, but dis is de famous Dominica mountain chicken, is a real delicticasy," Mr. Lamb said, surprised that we were not familiar with his supposedly famous dish.

Going to the corner he picked up two broomsticks, with three-inch nails bound tightly to the ends, and smiling expansively he handed them to two of our men.

"You got to jook de frogs you want to eat and give dem to me."

I watched in amusement as they engaged in this bizarre activity. The men tried to spear the big frogs through the mesh and whenever they managed to jab one, Mr. Lamb politely removed it from the end of the stick and took it away to be cooked. The ladies in the group politely declined, saying they would leave it to the 'boys.' The 'boys' found it wasn't as easy as it looked. The agile frogs were definitely not about to sit around and get skewered, and they hopped around making loud "rib-bit" noises, cleverly avoiding the deadly stick.

The men worked up quite a sweat as they jabbed away, doing double-duty to catch ones for their wives. They prevailed over the fast-moving frogs in the end and returned to their seats.

As the rum took effect, no one seemed to bother much about the swarms of biting mosquitoes buzzing about and our guests sat at their table and waited for the waitresses to bring their cooked mountain chicken. The frog legs were fried and tasted just like small chicken drumsticks. The steel band banged away and I was beginning to get a little impatient, when Mr. Lamb announced that the show was about to begin.

The long awaited Venus finally appeared on the stage, amidst a fanfare of whistles and clapping hands. She was a beautifully shaped young woman with skin black as ebony, attired in a very skimpy bikini studded with hundreds of coloured sparkling sequins, and her gold capped teeth sparkled when she smiled.

Venus began dancing around the small concrete floor while two assistants brought out a flaming limbo stick. With the encouragement of the audience, she managed to navigate this at an impossibly low level. After this she jumped to the sandy floor searching the audience for an unsuspecting helper. I managed to leap behind the bamboo partition with my two sons just in time. We watched from this position as Venus pounced on one of our unfortunate charter guests and dragged him to the dance floor, where she gyrated seductively, much to his embarrassment. The other men found this tremendously amusing, but the wives weren't looking any too happy and glared venomously at Venus.

Finally, the steel band slowed to a steady beat and Venus's two assistants placed a white canvas tarpaulin on the circular dance floor in the centre of the

Spotlight. They then made a round of the restaurant with two cardboard boxes, collecting the empty beer, rum, and wine bottles that had been consumed during the evening (which amounted to quite a few).

As we looked on in amazement, they broke the bottles into a deadly mass of jagged edges, and with pieces of cardboard they swept this to the centre of the stage. The jagged glass could clearly be seen from where we were sitting and there was no evidence of concealment or chicanery on anyone's part.

We watched apprehensively now, and many must have felt as I did. Surely this Venus woman would injure herself horribly if she went near that pile of glass? The steel band picked up momentum again and then without warning, Venus suddenly jumped into the glass. There was a cry of horror from everyone, even though this had been somewhat expected. When she actually jumped barefoot onto the razor sharp glass nobody could believe their eyes. The band beat a fast lively rhythm and Venus danced away. Her feet stomped up and down in the glass and she wiggled and squirmed while clapping her hands. There was no hesitation on her part and she actually seemed to be enjoying it, smiling and laughing all the while.

She put a wooden chair on the stage and stood on it before leaping down into the glass again. It was an unbelievable event to watch, but there was no denying the fact that she was dancing barefoot on a pile of broken glass and, it seemed, without getting cut.

She then made her most audacious move. Her two assistants were strong looking men of good stature and probably weighed a bit. Venus laid down in the broken glass and writhed around while one of the assistants stood on her stomach. He was a sensible fellow and was wearing shoes.

To this day, I cannot tell you how this woman managed her act without being horribly injured. After the show, Venus went from table to table displaying her smooth unblemished skin to all. Some of us went to check the glass as they were cleaning it up, only to find it was real enough.

As the years went by and I continued to sail the Windward Islands, I took many people to the Spotlight Restaurant in Portsmouth and we were always amazed by the bottle dance. Later, Mr. Lamb's place unfortunately burned down and I never saw him again. No one that I knew in the islands ever heard what happened to the mysterious Venus or where she went, but she certainly had an unusual talent. I am still baffled, but there are some things in life that just can't be explained.

In 1974, Lou, Peter, and I were privileged to see the last of the Bequia whalers in the course of their work. Amongst the first settlers of this Grenadine island were the Scottish and English seafarers, who hunted the great whales that sought solace in the lee of the Windward Islands. It was not uncommon in those years to see great pods of sperm whales resting on the surface in the calms to the west of the most mountainous islands.

A legacy passed down from generation to generation, the Bequia men pursued this holdover from another time in the traditional way. They hunted the great whales in wooden craft propelled by sail and oar, striking with hand held harpoons.

The stout double-ended wooden whaleboats were built on Bequia's shores by shipwrights wielding adze and hatchets handed down from father to son and grandson. There was never a paper design or line drawing to consult. The whalers of the day were built from memory and the clean line of hull, which had been captured by an unknown seafarer's eye so long ago, emerged again and again, faultlessly reproducing the type. Smooth grey hulls with black bottoms, they all sported a jib and huge spritsail to drive them through the chop. The heavy hand harpoons lay near the bows ready to do their duty when called upon.

The Bequia whalers of 1974 were a dying breed. The new generation worshipped the red Datsun taxi cab and the Sony tape deck. The squinting eye of strong men scanning the western horizon for the blow of whale would soon disappear.

We had often seen the whalers during our voyages, sailing the long tack in the lee of St. Vincent, and on other occasions we had seen the whales. Now we were to see the two joined in their primitive hunt.

The schooner *Janeen* lay on the starboard tack under four lowers, jib topsail and fisherman, steering a northerly course. We had just finished a charter in Union Island and were on our way back to St. Lucia. As we came into the lee of St. Vincent, we lost the strong tradewinds, but the big steel schooner was a great "ghoster" and we made good use of the light puffs coming down the valleys of the island. I had discovered over the years that during the winter months the wind could take a northerly slant, making for a hard windward slog along the island chain. So we hugged the rugged coast in order to get a high or windward start on the next open channel.

We saw the two whaleboats ahead, tiny white sails on a rich blue sea some three miles distant. They were close hauled, as we were, making to the north in the bright sunlight. The sea to the west of St. Vincent enjoys a fine lee, and the rough seas that are so common in the open channels between the islands do not penetrate here.

The *Janeen* overhauled the two smaller craft quickly, but when we saw whales spouting ahead of them, I decided to reduce sail and witness this event, surely amongst the last of the great whale hunts. We lowered away main and jib, and with main staysail and jumbo we stood off watching.

There were eight men in each boat, two of whom stood to windward, hiking from the single shroud. The harpooner stood forward, and with his arm, directed the man at the tiller to follow the huge sperm whales ahead of them. The other four hiked out on the windward rail in an effort to keep the craft on an even keel.

We watched as they slowly gained on their prey, and when they were within a hundred yards, both boats lowered their masts and sails, changing to oars. The pod of four sperm whales dove, leaving their seemingly puny pursuers on an empty sea, only to surface again some yards ahead.

We followed the hunters and their prey at a distance. The lead boat pulled on, and in the bow stood a man of some stout proportion, a long steel harpoon balanced easily in his hand. For a moment I felt a twinge of sadness, but I could not say if it was for the whalers or the whales. Both, it seemed to me, had laid a course towards extinction.

We watched from some two hundred yards as, with wild shouts, the lead boat struck the biggest of the sperm whales, a dark skinned fifty-footer. The great leviathan came to the surface ahead of the whaler and after blowing hard, bowed its back to dive once more. It almost seemed as though it had presented itself for the kill. Through the binoculars I saw the harpoon as it left the harpooner's hand and flew true to strike the broad curved back.

The whale thrashed mightily and sounded in a mist of spray. The whaleboat slacked out line, but after a moment the harpooner took a turn on the stern post and we watched as they were pulled along at a very fast rate. It was not long, however, before the whale came to the surface again, but this time the blow was deep red. The lance had penetrated the lungs and the huge mammal was dying even as it struggled to escape its tiny tormentors. We closed the distance along with the other whale boat as the great whale sounded again and again, each time for a shorter period. Inevitably, exhaustion overwhelmed the creature and it came to the surface for the last time. The hunters closed in, striking with the bigger lances.

Finally, the whaleboat came alongside the weakly struggling sperm whale and the first harpooner boarded its back, holding the long deadly killing lance. He stood on the whale's back in a spreading sea of blood, and as the whale blew for its final time, he was bathed in red. As I watched him raise his powerful arm to deal the final strike, I was taken back to the most primeval of times when man existed in his most basic forms, that of the hunter-killer.

We cracked on sail afterwards and made our way north under the shadow of the Soufriere volcano, which had recently threatened eruption. I felt that we had witnessed a conflict that few would see again. I could not judge the right or the wrong of it: that was beyond my own conscience. I was only a bystander. In only a few more years, the last of the men who had struck steel to living whales had gone, and there were none with the passion or the strength to pit themselves against nature in such a way. For better or for worse, it is no more.

One time, I sailed the *Janeen* to the beautiful Grenadines of the Windward Islands. Lou and Peter were aboard and we had a total of eleven crew. We were there to pick up Mr. Sprague and his party of eight. He was one of my repeat clients and had sailed with me for a number of years. He was a successful businessman who loved to sail, and usually chartered the boat for three or four weeks. There were always interesting people in his party, and two of his regulars were Mr. and Mrs. Sichel, owners of a wine company. We always knew when they were coming aboard, because weeks before the cruise, a dozen cases of wine would arrive into St. Lucia. We would take the schooner up to Castries Harbour to pick them up, and the crew would stow them in the storeroom below the galley.

Mr. Sichel was a gourmet and kept the chef on his toes during these trips. Only the very finest and the freshest was served. Mr. Sichel spent quite a bit of time in the galley offering snippets of advice to the chef, who was remarkably patient and understanding.

The schooner's deck crew were mostly West Indian and there were some good spear fishermen amongst them, including Lou and Peter. At many anchorages in the islands, they would go out early in the morning for an hour or so with their spear guns. They usually came back with something tasty to eat, quite often, lobsters. Conch were plentiful in many places and we dove down to the beds of turtle grass to pick up the big shells whenever we could. We all seemed to love conch chowder.

Mr. Sprague often went along on these expeditions to try his hand at the spear fishing and became pretty adept at it. In subsequent years, he arrived on the schooner equipped with the most modern spear guns available. Big compressed air jobs that could kill a whale. He shot some big fish on these trips and, of course, he had a lot of fun.

The shipwreck incident occurred during one of the Sprague charters. The Sichels were guests that year, along with Nirhavani Nirhavana, a champion wrestler from Iran. It was a three week charter from Martinique to Grenada. Mr. Nirhavana arrived with a large igloo cooler, full to brimming with little blue cans of Iranian caviar, the ones with the rubber bands around them. He also brought along a case of vodka to have with his fish eggs.

During the second week of the cruise, we anchored in the lovely Tobago Cays. Even though this was one of the favourite anchorages of the day, it was still unusual to find more than one or two yachts there at any one time, and we were often alone.

Horseshoe and World's End Reef surrounded the four tiny cays providing protection from the Atlantic swell. A favourite anchorage of the Spragues', they often requested we stay there for a number of days to snorkel on the coral reef. We were not on any kind of schedule, so would always oblige.

One evening, while our guests sat aft sipping cocktails, Lou, Peter, and I were chatting up forward, enjoying a small rum before dinner. We noticed that a sail had appeared north east of Horseshoe Reef. I picked up the binoculars to have a closer look. It was a small sloop on a southwesterly course and certainly in an odd position for that time of day. Her skipper would have a hard time seeing the reef ahead of them because the sun was low in the sky and right in their eyes.

We were concerned that if the sloop did not change course quickly, she would hit the reef. It was not a particularly rough day, but the water on the eastern side of that coral had a few thousand miles of open ocean behind it, and there was a long low swell rolling in.

Sure enough, as we watched through the glasses, the little sloop hit and bounced up over the reef, coming to rest on a shallow patch of coral. Although it was late in the day, I decided to send Lou and Peter off in the motor gig to help. This was a twenty-two-foot wooden craft with an outboard motor, which could be rowed or sailed, and so, with another of the deckhands they took off. It was a good three quarters of a mile to the stranded vessel.

Darkness was falling as they headed out to the reef, but as I looked through the binoculars I saw some activity on the stranded sloop. Suddenly, an orange life-raft popped up alongside it. As the motor gig got closer, the life-raft drifted downwind towards them and soon they were alongside it.

Lou told me later that they found a man inside the raft, in what seemed to be a state of shock. He was unable to speak and sat on the floor of the raft shaking.

"Are you alright?" Lou asked him concerned.

He responded by nodding his head. They lifted him out by the arms and set him down in the bottom of the gig out of the wind. He was wet and cold.

They dragged the life-raft up over the bow and then brought the shipwreck survivor back to the schooner. It was dark by then, but we got him aboard and laid the life-raft on the foredeck of the *Janeen*.

We took him down to a cabin and gave him some dry clothes, coffee, and a hot dinner, which he ate. He was dazed and very quiet and we figured that he was probably an amateur sailor who was taking this misadventure very hard. I was below trying to talk to the poor chap when Lou called me up on deck.

"Skipper, what do you make of that?" he asked pointing out towards the reef where the wrecked sloop lay. Someone was waving a flashlight slowly back and forth.

"Looks like there's someone still on the boat," I said to Lou. "You'd better get back out there and find out what's going on."

I had been around long enough to know that it wasn't going to be easy to get to the sloop in the dark, but the wind had died down a bit with nightfall, as it usually did in those latitudes, and the swell would be down as well. Lou and Peter set off again, accompanied by two deckhands this time, and a pair of powerful torch lights.

Working their way cautiously through the shallow reef towards the wreck, they were amazed to hear a woman's voice.

"Help! Help me please!"

She was waving the flashlight, which was lucky indeed because it was very dark and they would have had the devil's own time trying to find her otherwise.

"We're coming. Hold on," Peter reassured her.

They picked their way carefully through the coral heads with the two torch lights until they were at the wreck. The deckhands fended off the port and starboard bows with oars, while Lou and Peter did the same from the stern. They managed to get the gig right up to the stranded sloop without damage and, sure enough, there was a woman in a yellow life jacket sitting on the lee side of the boat and very glad to see them.

They took her aboard and made their way back out through the reef. Soon they were motoring back towards the *Janeen*. They gave the poor shivering woman a towel, and through chattering teeth she told them their story. They were Americans and newcomers to the islands, cruising on their new forty-footer. Their misfortune had been a result of inexperience and a bit of bad judgment. She then burst into tears and told them about her husband, whom she had last seen in the cockpit just before the sloop hit the reef. She had fallen down the companionway and hit her head, knocking herself out. When she finally came around, her husband was gone.

"Bob must have drowned when the boat hit," she wailed tearfully.

"But your husband is alive," Lou told her. "He's on our schooner. We picked him up in the life-raft."

"The life-raft?" she said looking puzzled.

"Yes, you know, the life-raft from your boat," Lou explained to her.

The grief she had been feeling for the loss of her husband turned to joy and her tears disappeared. Yet even as our second survivor climbed the boarding ladder, she was putting two and two together. Safely on the deck she suddenly exploded.

"You rotten sonofabitch," she howled. "Where are you?" Luckily for her husband, he was still in shock down below in the crew's mess hall.

"You bastard! You left me out there."

She was really screaming now, while scanning the dimly lit faces on deck to see if she could recognize her hubby.

The fact that her husband had jumped off in the survival raft, leaving her on the wreck to fend for herself incensed her and she spat out exactly what she was going to do to him when she found him. It wasn't going to be very pretty. I was just glad I wasn't in his shoes. In all my born days, I have never seen anyone so angry.

We felt it prudent to keep them apart that night and arranged bunks for them in different areas of the ship. Our charter party took it all in stride and eventually we all went to bed.

The next day the police boat came up from the island of Union and the sloop was pulled off with little damage. The two survivors left us there, still not speaking to one another.

Our cruise ended in Grenada, and a sun-tanned and content Sprague party flew out to their various destinations around the world. I was happy too. Nirhavani left a number of the tins of Iranian caviar in the igloo and it was not long before I was shovelling large spoonfuls of the succulent black fish eggs blissfully into my mouth.

Passages

THE *JANEEN* CONTINUED TO CHARTER and I followed the sea, but the winds of change were once again blowing, and there were events looming on the horizon that would have a bearing on our lives.

Lou and Peter had become skippers by now and even Brian was on the sea road as well, as first mate on a big Swedish three-masted square rigger.

In 1975 we got an offer for the *Janeen*. I had not listed her for sale, so it came as a surprise. Some wealthy Italians had seen her and decided they wanted her for themselves. I told them she was not for sale, but they made us such a high offer, we felt we couldn't refuse. So the *Janeen* sailed out of our lives and although we were saddened to see her go, the wonderful memories remained with us, and these perhaps are more valuable than the teak and the steel itself.

Many years later, this lovely schooner was completely rebuilt and re-christened *Mariette*, the name she still sails under today.

I was nearing my sixties by then and for the first time I had to admit I was no longer young. When I looked in the mirror I saw a face creased and weathered by a life under sail. The wrinkles were deep, the grey hair thinning, and my skin the colour of old tanned leather.

Terry and I talked about our lives and our future. Was it time to retire? But we both knew the answer to that. I would continue to go to sea and Terry would stand by me. A man who has spent his whole life on the ocean cannot easily change, and she understood I would be lost without a ship to sail.

So, we began looking for another vessel to continue our charter business. Through the yacht brokers we heard about a lovely eighty-foot Philip Rhodes steel ketch for sale in the Balearic Islands, and so Lou and I flew to Spain to look at her. She was laying at her berth in the Club de Mar in Palma. A pretty steel hulled vessel, with a centreboard that would allow us to cruise in shallow areas, like the Bahamas. The agent took us aboard for an inspection. There were generously sized cabins for six guests and crews' quarters for six. There was a captain's cabin as well. She was powered with a six cylinder General Motors diesel and a twelve KW generator.

The yacht was called *Giralda* and owned by Don Juan de Bourbon, the Count of Barcelona, and father of Juan Carlos, the King of Spain. During our negotiations, Don Juan invited us to dine with him at the Royal Club Nautico. We were instructed to wait at the entrance of the club, so he could enter before us. We turned up at the appointed time and a moment later Don Juan and his personal captain arrived and we followed them in.

The Royal Club Nautico was an impressive old building with high teak panelled walls and rich red carpets. Walking through these august hallways to the

GIRALDA WAS A FAST SAILER, AND WON
THE ST. PETERSBURG – HAVANA RACE ONE YEAR.

dining room, I marvelled at the wonderful collection of nautical oil paintings. His Highness walked first, followed by his captain, then myself, with Lou bringing up the rear. Entering the dining room, we passed numerous other diners on our way to the royal table. They rose in turn, bowing or curtsying. His Highness and I returned the friendly gestures with salutes, and the folks seemed so friendly that I added a few "How do you do's" and "Good evenings." Lou later told me that he felt like giving me a swift kick in the arse then. He said they were honouring His Highness and not me. We sat down and in between mouthfuls, talked of the sea and sailing ships. Eventually we struck a deal with regard to the sale of the yacht.

Painting her hull a royal blue, we renamed her *High Barbaree*, after the Barbaree pirates of North Africa, and an artist inscribed this in gold leaf on her transom. Before leaving Spain, Lou and I had one last adventure.

It was a well known fact that there were longstanding animosities between Don Juan and General Franco, and it all came to a head while we were there. Don Juan made some remarks regarding the Spanish monarchy's views on democracy and Franco gave Don Juan forty-eight hours to get out of Spain. He also gave orders to seize all of Don Juan's assets in Spain, which technically included our ship. We had paid for the yacht in full by then, but we were still awaiting the final release documents. Don Juan waved to us as he lit out of Palma, bound for Portugal, leaving us moored in the royal berth. I could not believe we had gotten ourselves into such a mess.

Lou and I decided to make a run for the French coast. I was not about to have the Spanish government appropriate our ship. We had just paid a lot of dollars for her and I was upset at being left holding the bag of beans.

The following night Lou struck up a conversation with the guard who was watching the yacht. He gave him the bottle of strong West Indian rum we had been saving for a special occasion. Later that night, when he was well and truly sauced, we made ready to slip our lines. The guard was most obliging by then, and weaving around the dock bollards, he managed to cast our lines off. He even waved us goodbye as we made our way out of the Club de Mar Marina. Setting sail, we made the run to Antibes and felt all the better once we were moored there. At least General Franco would not be able to lift my ship. Later on, though, we received the releases from the agent in Palma, signed by Franco himself, giving us permission to take the ship out of Spanish waters.

Peter and Terry joined us and we sailed the *High Barbaree* out of the Mediterranean, West Indies-bound. We had a slow and windless passage of twenty-four days across the Atlantic, but finally we arrived in our home cruising grounds and we anchored once again in the lagoons of Marigot Bay.

WITH LOU AND TERRY, THE DAY BEFORE WE LEFT ST. THOMAS FOR FLORIDA.

It was then that we decided to sell the hotel. It had been a lot of work for Terry to manage, and frankly we had seen little profit after all was said and done. Terry would sail with me as chef and I was happy at the prospect. So, we sold the Yacht Haven Hotel to a company called The Moorings, who still own it today and run their popular bareboat charter business from there.

With our crew of six, we sailed *High Barbaree* to far-flung ports across the world and our adventures continued. Terry and I chartered together for a number of years in every area of the Caribbean from Venezuela to the northern Bahamas. We sailed to the Mediterranean and the eastern United States. Terry excelled at her new position of chef and we were both very happy. We were proving that even at our age, there could be new beginnings.

In the early eighties, we decided to sail the *High Barbaree* north from the West Indies to Florida. Lou came to help us and we looked forward to an enjoyable voyage. We had been planning this trip through the Bahamas to Florida for a couple of years, as our vessel needed repair work which could only be undertaken in Miami. So, when our charter season in the Virgin Islands came to a close in May, we decided to head north.

It was a time when there were rampant rumours about drug pirates in the Bahamas, but there were documented statistics sufficient to cause anxiety in the sailing community. Many yachts, both large and small, chose to carry firearms in order to defend themselves. We were no exception.

Prior to leaving, we consulted with U.S. coast guard officers in St. Thomas, who gave us an update on the situation and what precautions yachts should take.

"Drug smugglers find it easy to hit yachts and use them for transport," they said. "Yachtsmen are too naive and tend to put themselves in harm's way. Be prepared and alert at all times."

They also gave us a little background as to how the "pirates" operated, and how best for us not to get ourselves into trouble.

According to them, a hijacking could take many different forms and depended largely on the circumstances. But, of the cases so far recorded, there were a number of chilling examples.

The most common *modus operandi* was to attack a yacht in the open sea, where there would be no witnesses. They would come alongside in a fast boat, kill the people onboard, and take over the yacht. The Bahamas lent itself well to this method of attack because of the vast expanses of calm, sheltered water, a place where yachts on passage could be found alone.

Another reported method was to set a trap for their prey by placing a life-raft in the path of an oncoming yacht, with some armed pirates posing as shipwreck survivors inside. A distress flare might be used to lure the yacht to the raft. When the flare is spotted, the captain calls all hands on deck. What excitement, there may be someone in need of help! The yacht changes course toward the flare and the life-raft is sighted. For many of the crew aboard the yacht, this is an exhilarating experience. They line the rail as the raft come alongside and two rough-looking "survivors" suddenly jump up with guns in hand. There is no problem in dispatching the yacht crew, they have conveniently lined themselves up along the rail, like targets at a shooting gallery. There had been other cases where yachts have anchored alone in secluded anchorages and disappeared.

Everyone agreed that these Bahamian-based drug smugglers were a serious problem, and to a lesser degree were a danger in the other areas of the West Indies. Over the past few years many yachts and vessels had just disappeared, while others were found abandoned under mysterious circumstances. Many of the crews of these yachts had just vanished, but there were grim press releases telling of bullet-ridden bodies being washed up on secluded shores. There were a few survivors too, who lived to tell of their horrible ordeals.

According to the authorities, drugs entering the United States took many different routes. Traditionally, the bulk of this traffic came by sea using the old Yucatan Channel into the Gulf of Mexico, where it dispersed to the many gulf ports of the southern United States. But, as the war on drugs escalated, the U.S. government made it increasingly difficult for the smugglers to use this route, so they began seeking other avenues to channel their drugs north. As a result, more and more traffic flowed to the eastern side of the Caribbean Sea, to make its way north along the island chain.

It is interesting to note that the northern section of the Bahamas is included in the mysterious "Bermuda Triangle." Case files of yachts and ships lost in this area have often been closed with nothing more than "missing, presumed lost at sea" printed on the folder. Personally, I believe that the main reason for the higher numbers of maritime disappearances in this area can be chalked up to the very high density of marine traffic there. But drug smugglers would find it very convenient having any ships or yachts they sink in the Gulf Stream being reported as "Lost in the Bermuda Triangle."

Quite often a yacht would be hijacked for the last leg of the smuggling trip only. A long range motor fishing vessel would be used to bring the drugs from the point of origin to within a day's run from the desired port of entry. It goes without saying that a foreign-flagged fishing vessel approaching the east coast of Florida would be far more suspect than, say, a forty-foot yacht approaching under normal circumstances. A yacht could enter port, discharge its cargo secretly and then put to sea again, and be sunk in the open waters without anyone knowing.

The cocaine trade required the development of a specialized type of boat, which we began to see in the impoundment yards at police stations and coast guard bases throughout the area. These craft were often converted pleasure cruisers fitted with huge engines and fuel tanks. They were usually in the thirty foot range and of the deep V offshore type. Very large outboards, of 250 horsepower or so, or inboard engines of at least equal power, are the norm. With long range fuel tanks and speeds in the vicinity of fifty knots, the local authorities found them hard to detect or catch using their own much slower and less sophisticated equipment.

These high-speed drug boats were used because the weight of the cocaine cargo was negligible. Then there were the larger craft, the trawlers, small cargo vessels, and other commercial types in which the smugglers tried to sneak through under the guise of conducting legal business. These vessels would carry large quantities of marijuana, a bulkier cargo.

I resolved that we would arm ourselves sufficiently well, so we could protect ourselves in case of an attack. This may sound a little melodramatic, but I wanted to make sure that we didn't become an addition to the missing persons' list.

So, we took stock of our armoury. I had onboard an old single shot .22 calibre rifle and a very small ladies .32 calibre star pistol. The St. Thomas coast guard officer politely pointed out that these pop guns were wholly inadequate for the protection of a yacht. He recommended we stock up with some real guns that would give us a chance to fight back, if it ever came to that. He also remarked that the drug pirates are always able to buy more numerous bigger and better guns than a yachtsman would. The key to it, he said, was that the pirates don't want to die. They want to be around to enjoy their ill-gotten gains. So, if a situation appeared where their "victims" were well-armed and prepared to fight, the pirates might be less enthusiastic about attempting a hijacking. The officer added that if firearms were going to be a part of our inventory, we should know how to use them and have them accessible at all times. It would be no good shouting, "Honey, where did we stow the bullets?" as the attackers came barrelling down the hatch!

WE WERE ARMED AND READY, AND THAT FACT PROBABLY SAVED OUR LIVES.

So, we bought a selection of guns. We secured a 9 mm Mauser infantry rife from a German yachtsman who was selling his boat. From a local security firm we purchased one twelve gauge semi-automatic shotgun, one .308 Remington hunting rifle and one .45 calibre pistol, plus a whole lot of ammunition.

The month of May saw us en route to Florida with nine souls aboard. We lost no time learning how to use our guns and each crew member fired numerous rounds at empty containers thrown from the bow. The firearms were kept secured in the pilot-house with ready ammunition.

The *High Barbaree* made a fast passage from the Virgins to Great Inagua and apart from one night, just north of Tortuga, when we encountered some very high seas, we enjoyed fine weather.

A day later we passed west of Acklins and Crooked Island. There was no wind and we powered north at about seven-and-a-half knots with no sail set.

The following morning, a dark green trawler appeared about five miles astern of us on a course some forty degrees to the east of ours. After half an hour, she came around to match our course. About three miles away she lined up astern and her bow wave rose as she cracked on speed. Beginning to worry, I called all hands on deck and we took turns looking through the binoculars.

Long Island lay to the southwest and although we could see the shore, there was no chance of making any landfall, as there were no safe harbours on the windward side of the island, and so we motored on.

As the trawler approached to within three hundred yards, we picked out the details on her deck. She was seventy-five or eighty-feet-long and resembled the wooden types built in the southern United States for the gulf shrimp fishery. The pilot-house was situated forward, aft of which stood the steel fishing masts and rigging. Vessels of this type and size were usually fitted with big diesels and could make a good ten to twelve knots.

No one was visible, but we saw the periodic flash of binocular lenses through the pilot-house windows. Her fishing booms were out but they were not pulling any nets. However, the vessel appeared to have a full load as she was sitting low in the water.

At two hundred yards our pursuer slowed down, and for the next hour held her distance. We altered course to see if she would follow and she matched our every move. I ordered our weapons out and we carefully loaded them, putting extra ammunition aside. It was just like the drills we had conducted and everyone knew what to do.

I felt anxious, unable to believe this could possibly be happening. For the first time in my life I was faced with the possibility of losing a vessel under my command. But by pirates? This was a hard one to come to grips with.

Gone was the usual light banter between the crew. We were all silent now, and the sound of the main engine exhaust seemed very loud in our ears.

Towards mid afternoon, the trawler began closing the distance between us and we increased speed to about eight-and-a-half knots, which was as fast as we could go. It had developed into one of those hot Bahamian days with a clear sky, flat sea, and not a breath of wind.

We would get no help from our sails, so we left them furled. I was dubious as to how long our trusty but ageing engine was going to hold up at full throttle. We were still a long way away from Rum Cay, where we planned to spend the night.

When she was two-hundred-and-fifty feet off, we saw three or four people in the pilot-house of the trawler looking at us through binoculars. A bearded man stepped briefly outside, giving us a quick look before ducking back in.

There was no doubt by this time that the trawler was attempting to do something, but I still found it hard to believe they were actually going to try and hijack us. Then we all saw something that really put the fear of God into us. The bearded man stepped out again, but this time he had a gun cradled in his arms. He stood at the rail looking at us, talking back into the pilot-house. It was almost as if he wanted us to see that he was armed.

We had to do something then. Whatever it was they were going to do, they were getting ready to do it and we couldn't run fast enough to get away. I spoke quickly to Lou and then all of the armed crew of the *High Barbaree* moved to the after deck with their guns in hand, while I stayed at the wheel.

Those armed with a rifle or shotgun held them above their heads with both hands, while those with hand guns held them aloft in one hand. I had the .45 calibre pistol at the wheel, while Randy, the engineer, held the shotgun aloft. Jim held a shotgun and Barnard the .308. Terry took the small .32 calibre pistol and bravely waved it aloft. Lou stood by the rail with the big Mauser, adjusting the sights.

We displayed our guns openly and clearly, so the crew of the trawler could see them. My crew was ready to jump for cover should anyone in the trawler make a threatening move. The drug trawler (which we were now convinced it was) held its position two hundred feet astern of us. After displaying the weapons, our crew returned to the relative shelter of the steel cockpit coaming and waited. We decided that if the trawler approached any closer, we would fire at its bow.

Our vessel was equipped with VHF radio and although we had been trying to raise someone for some hours now, we weren't able to get through to anyone.

Late in the afternoon, there was activity on the trawler and she speeded up, coming closer. We opened fire. I aimed from behind the steel coaming and at the same time the shotgun and .308 barked from the other side of the cockpit. Lou knelt on the port side and fired the Mauser. A frightened but determined Terry stood in the companionway holding the .32 in her hand. We aimed for the bow of the trawler at waterline level, and while the two rifles were hitting that general area, the shotgun was raising splashes of water wildly around her bow. We quickly fired off more than twenty rounds each and the rifle barrels became pretty hot. The crew of the trawler did not return fire, but they slowed down, dropping back to a respectable distance. We stopped firing.

We were not trained soldiers and it was a strange feeling indeed to be firing these powerful and dangerous weapons at something other than an empty oil can, but at the same time we knew that our lives were in peril.

There was a respite then, until towards dusk when we began to close the island of Rum Cay. The trawler made another attempt then and came to within one hundred feet. We fired again. I knew we were hitting the bow of the wooden trawler this time as we could see the splinters of wood fly as each shot hit. The shotgun buck was hitting her bow this time too, leaving large areas of bare wood, but the bullets caused little damage to the heavily constructed vessel.

This time the bearded man on the trawler fired back. Three times he jumped out from the safety of his pilot-house, firing wild bursts from his automatic weapon.

"Fire at the pilot-house!" I shouted.

None of the bullets from the trawler had hit us as yet, but it would take only one. I watched as Lou aimed carefully and as he fired, one of the glass windows in the trawler's pilot-house exploded in a shower of broken glass. They were no more than seventy-five feet from our stern now.

"Keep firing," I yelled. "Don't stop."

I felt we must give it our all now and try to keep the men from being able to fire at us at such close range. The twelve gauge shotgun found its mark now too and another of the pilot-house windows burst inwards. The men on the trawler hid inside, but they continued to fire at us and we ducked as a short burst hit our stern and the mizzen mast. The bullets hitting the steel made a quick ping, ping, ping, surprisingly like the sound one hears in the movies. But this was no movie, it was real.

Some finger-sized chunks of varnished spruce fell to the deck around us where they had hit the mizzen mast. We continued to fire at the trawler until our ammunition was almost exhausted. When buying the shells in St. Thomas, I never realized quite how quickly they could be used. We fired a few final rounds as the trawler backed off and stopped firing at us. They would never know how close we had come to running out of bullets.

As dusk fell, we closed the last mile to Rum Cay and the trawler finally broke away, altering course to the north. We were terribly shaken by this ordeal, although it didn't affect us until after it was over and we had put our weapons down. We could see the lights of two other yachts anchored in Rum Cay and made radio contact with one of them as we approached the anchorage. We put on the spreader lights and were amazed at the number of shell casings littering the aft deck.

At the last moment, the *High Barbaree*, its engine overheating and its crew shaken but relieved, sped into the bay and the green trawler continued steaming away to the north. We later surmised that they may have been waiting for darkness before making their move.

We anchored and squared away for the night, leaving the generator running to kept the yacht well lit up. The crew from the other two yachts came aboard and we told them our tale. They also left their lights on and one even moved nearer, so we were all close together. Inspecting the engine room, I found the main engine had boiled out most of its water and been close to burning itself up. We could not have carried on for much longer.

As tired as we were, none of us could sleep that night and I sat on deck talking with Terry until the early hours of the morning, and thinking about what had just taken place. I had no idea how close the trawler had come to ramming us, but I felt a little chill run down my spine as I considered what might have been. I thought back to my time on the *Angelus*. That was the last and only other occasion anyone had pointed a gun at me. One thing for sure was that they had been deterred by our show of strength and our willingness to fight back. I know that everyone aboard the *High Barbaree* was scared that day, but I also know that if the drug pirates had tried to board our vessel, they would have had a real fight on their hands. As we finally went below to sleep, I felt my age. I was certainly too old to be fighting drug pirates.

There is a satisfying end to this story. A few days later, we saw the green trawler again in the bight of Eleuthera. On this occasion, she was tied up alongside a large white U.S. coast guard cutter. We called them on the radio, but they wouldn't divulge much about the trawler, other than to say it was involved in illegal activities. They seemed preoccupied and not very interested in our story, which I found surprising, although we did find it difficult trying to relay all the details on the VHF.

We saw the trawler one last time on the television in Fort Lauderdale, having been arrested with millions of dollars of drugs on board, and its Colombian crew had been charged.

Hurricane!

THE WORD HURRICANE IS WELL KNOWN to mariners, and we have learned to respect and fear these cyclonic storm systems for the death and destruction they can bring. Legend holds that the ancient Carib Indians of the Eastern Caribbean feared their god "Hurracan" above all others, and would sacrifice young virgins to avoid his wrath. While we knew a few chaps in the charter business who would probably have liked to carry on this practice, we relied more on radio weather reports.

The West Indian hurricane season runs from July to October, as illustrated by this piece of doggerel, coined by some unknown seaman: June—too soon, July—rely, August—a must, September—remember, October—all over. The late September storms traditionally seemed to be the most dangerous, and it was one of these that almost took the *High Barbaree* from us.

Of course there had been hurricanes over the years, but through luck and wit we had managed to avoid serious damage. The *Ramona* survived a blow in Florida one year, while moored up the Miami River. Later the *Janeen* weathered a storm within the protection of Marigot Bay. We hid the *Caribee* in Hatchet Bay, Eleuthera one year, but we had never suffered a direct hit by a full-blown hurricane.

We learned early on that one had to follow each low carefully as it crossed the Atlantic, monitoring its day-to-day progress. During the initial years of the charter business, good weather reports were rare birds. Our one ace had been the telephone number for the National Hurricane Centre in Miami, Florida. We could place long-distance calls there to get up-to-the-minute information. This was often our only reliable source. The local island meteorological offices were not much help, as evidenced by a call I made to the St. Lucia bureau one day in the early seventies.

"I'm leaving today, can you give me a weather report?" I asked.

"You mean how rough it is?" a female voice replied.

"Yes, I need to know what the forecast is."

"How big is your boat?"

"I don't know what that has to do with it, but she's 130 feet."

"Oh! well, dat's big enough, you could go."

Many of the Caribbean islands between Trinidad and Puerto Rico offered protected anchorages for the usual range of adverse weather conditions, but there were few "hurricane holes" where a vessel might find good shelter in a really bad blow. Marigot Bay was excellent, and this had been one of the reasons I had been drawn to that magical bay in the first place. In fact, when the Moorings Company bought our hotel, they renamed it the Hurricane Hole Hotel. There were few other eastern Caribbean harbours of equal quality in this respect.

The mid-eighties found us in St. Thomas. As our years advanced, Terry and I had found winter chartering in the Virgin Islands easier. Distances were much shorter and one could travel from anchorage to anchorage in only an hour or two. The islands and cays abounded in good anchorages and there were plenty of fine white sand beaches for our passengers. There were the occasional summer trips too, and we had just finished one of these when we began tracking a suspicious tropical depression in the eastern Atlantic.

The big low pressure system had drifted off the African coast a week before, gaining strength as it came over the Atlantic. The malevolent mass of thunderstorms and squalls made amazingly quick progress across the vast empty reaches of the ocean, staying for the most part near fourteen degrees latitude. We followed the weather reports carefully, and when it was still five hundred miles east of the Lesser Antilles, the tropical depression began its malignant metamorphosis.

For some unknown reason, the surface of the Atlantic ocean was a few degrees warmer than usual that year, and the system took sustenance from this. The air rose slowly, forming an eye and this started, almost imperceptibly, to spin. It was sluggish at first, but then ever so slowly it picked up speed. The vicious squalls and huge thunderheads strung out loosely throughout the system were pulled into the cyclonic spin, and orderly feeder-bands formed like long claws emanating from the eye. The storm grew in strength and continued on its course of almost due west.

We left the St. Thomas marina in the U.S. Virgin Islands that morning, steaming east. The storm was below us in latitude and to our east. Traditionally, tropical systems such as this always travelled west and they almost always curved north somewhere along their track. It was time for us to seek shelter. The only place where we could hope to find protection was in Coral Bay, St. John. This was a reasonably well protected series of bay and coves that while not as good as Marigot, would be the best in the U.S. Virgins. These lagoons had reasonably high bluffs and hills all around, which would hopefully cut the wind.

We arrived after three hours, and motored into the bay at speed to find ourselves a place. It was not as easy as one might surmise. There were many yachts in the islands by this time and everyone was determined to secure one of the better protected spaces. If you were casual about it and came late, you could find yourself without a suitable mooring spot. There were ten or so other vessels jostling for a space, but we were early and managed to secure one of the best spots in the innermost lagoon, next to three other large yachts.

We straddled both bow anchors at their extreme range and putting our stern to the mangrove tree-lined shore, we began to take hawsers ashore. These heavy warps were kept in the hold and lazarette for this purpose, so we brought them on deck and I had the crew walk them inland to a couple of large trees, where they were made fast. Each line was then parcelled against chaffing. We whipped the sails to the booms with small line, and anything on deck that could move was either lashed down or stowed below. I had learned that preparation was the answer in such situations and we made the most of the time we had.

The National Hurricane Centre in Miami issued hourly reports, and through the following day we listened carefully to the broadcasts. The tropical storm made the graduation to a hurricane only a hundred miles to the east of Barbados, and at the speed it was travelling, it hit the island with little advance warning.

Barbados was flat and her low-lying hills offered meagre protection from the hurricane's wrath. It passed directly over the island, ravaging the land and causing floods and considerable damage. Because it was so flat, Barbados had no adequate channels for heavy run off, and after the first few hours of torrential rains there were large areas of the island under a foot or more of water.

Seventy-mile-an-hour winds blasted the sugar cane plantations, flattening the tall stalks and ripping the sheet galvanized roofing from the small houses dotting the landscape. Where the wind was strongest, the sheets flew around like giant razor blades, threatening to slice in half anyone who got in the way.

The distance from Barbados to St. Lucia is only ninety miles, but this was enough of a run for the hurricane to strengthen even more before it rolled in on the high mountainous ridges of St. Lucia's volcanic backbone. It arrived with more torrential rains, and the deep ravines and rivers swelled into brown silt-laden torrents, staining the Caribbean a dirty brown many miles out. St. Lucia's rich red clay soil became waterlogged in places, and in more than one village people died as the water-laden hillsides came falling down in deadly mud slides. Bits of tree trunks and all kinds of flotsam and jetsam quickly littered the surface of the sea as the storm passed.

A day later, after leaving the coast of St. Lucia, the hurricane made the expected curve to the north, which put it on a path towards us. The winds surrounding the eye had by then increased to one-hundred-and-fifty knots, and I knew we would taste of this tempest's wrath. A line of vicious outlying squalls comprised the northernmost sector of the system, extending some hundred miles from the eye. This was the infamous "leading edge punch" of cyclonic systems, potentially the most dangerous half of the storm.

It was early afternoon as Terry and I stood on the *High Barbaree*'s deck looking towards the darkening sky far to the east.

"It sure looks ominous, Walter," she said to me.

"Probably just the first of it," I replied.

The line of squalls we were looking at were the outlying feeder bands, some hundred miles in front of the eye. They were weak compared to what would come later. The sky gradually grew overcast, and as the afternoon wore on the squalls closed the distance to St. John with surprising speed. By 5:30 P.M., the eastern sky was menacingly black.

The wind came in gusts of at least thirty knots, I estimated, and it picked the tops off the wavelets that had appeared in the lagoon, blowing spray into our faces. As the first line squall moved in on us, the cloud cover closed up and the last remnants of blue sky were blotted out. It was as if a huge dark blanket was being drawn over us. With the sun gone altogether it grew strangely dark, and the low scudding clouds dropped lower and lower until it seemed that we could reach up and touch the fast moving masses. I called the crew and we made a final thorough check of our anchors and stern lines. Once it started to blow there would be little we could do.

Night fell more quickly than usual, and a brilliant display of pyrotechnics appeared as the dark sky was lit by bolts of lightening. The eye of the hurricane was forecast to pass just a few miles to the south of us and the wind would initially blow into Coral Bay.

The *High Barbaree* began to roll strangely as gusts of wind caught the tops of her masts, and a low ominous drone emanated from beyond the clouds.

Mother Nature was about to vent her fury on us.

The first rain drops blew almost horizontally over Coral Bay, stinging our exposed skin, so without wasting any more time we went below. Total darkness fell then, and I felt it was going to be a long night. The wind rose steadily until it was gusting at seventy-five knots. Our vessel tore at her cables, wildly gyrating through eighty degrees. The wind shrieked through the rigging and the *High Barbaree* threatened to break free from her moorings.

By midnight, the mast top anemometer recorded a hundred-knot gust before it was blown away. The noise was terrifying, sounding like a score of freight trains roaring over us. The hurricane vented its fury with blasts of thunder that shook our hull as if the devil himself was trying to rend it. The hours of darkness dragged on and the hurricane raged. The eye came inexorably on, and the violently spinning wall of wind and rain approached St. John.

The wind began to make strange noises as it blew over the island. It was like blowing on the mouth of a bottle, I thought. The many openings and cracks in the rocky hills and bluffs acted like a giant organ and the stones of St. John vented their anguish in loud groans and shrieks.

The long low swell, which had begun to come in from the east had built in size until now there were forty-footers breaking and rolling in on the island's south coast. The huge seas hurled themselves on the shore, where their awesome power was broken into maelstroms of white frothy surf. We could almost feel the land tremble. As the wind rose to its peak in the early hours, the surf climbed higher and higher on the island's shores. Soon the surge was coming into Coral Bay.

The steel ketch rose and fell like a cork as frenzied seas entered the lagoon. Between the wind and the water I felt as though we were being batted by two huge demons. As each savage wall of wind hit us, I felt sure that we would be blown ashore, or worse, adrift. And then a wild wave would roll in to rush the *High Barbaree* to the extent of her cables.

Both anchors began to drag and the range of our movement increased. Of the fifteen heavy lines we had ashore, four had parted by midnight and the remaining newer ones sang like guitar strings when the vessel's eighty tons came up taut. We attempted to go onto the deck to check them, but it was impossible. The force of the wind was so great that we had to hold on with both hands to save ourselves from being taken away. The night was filled with flying debris and I feared that one of us might be blinded or blown overboard, so we returned to the relative safety of the wardroom where the crew huddled.

The blackness above us was illuminated again and again by brilliant forks of lightning and the smell of ozone pervaded the night. Flickering light penetrated the deck skylights playing strangely on our faces and blasts of thunder shook our bodies to the core. I had never experienced anything like this, I thought, raw nature in its most awesome form.

Through the early hours of the morning the hurricane raged on and the eye passed close south of us. The night seemed to go on forever, but by 4:00 A.M. I sensed there was a lessening in the fury. From that moment on there was gradual improvement.

The following morning broke clear, and going up on deck we surveyed our surroundings. Our decks were littered with leaves, branches, and other debris from the land, and looking ashore we could see that the tree branches were bereft of green. A twelve-foot dingy had been blown from the deck of a nearby yacht and was now lodged under our staysail boom.

Thankfully, we had come through without serious damage. It was to be our last summer in the Virgin Islands, and we would spend the coming years in the lower Caribbean. Without really knowing it, Terry and I were approaching the end of our voyaging together. In 1989 we decided to stop chartering. I was seventy by then, and my old bones were protesting the rigours of a life at sea.

A Sailor Gone

IT IS NOW 1994, AND THE YEARS HAVE FLOWN PAST like leaves on the wind. I am old now and near to the time when I will leave this world for another. My eyes no longer see as well as before, and my body is but a facsimile of the strong young man who went to sea over fifty years ago.

The years, however, have been kind to me and the pages of my book of life are filled to overflowing. All that remains is the reading and the savouring. The memories are strong and fine like a good wine, and nearly all that came to pass is as I would have wished.

It was my desire to come back once more to the place where it all began, and my daughter Janeen brought us to Baddeck. Terry follows as Janeen takes me by the hand. The waters of the Bras d'Or Lakes look just the same, although more than forty years have passed. We board the fisherman's lobster boat and go out to the cove. I see the shape of the *Yankee*'s hull, sitting just below the surface. She has rested there quietly since the day she sank so many years before. Later, Janeen takes me to the shore. It is evening and the summer sun sinks low on the hills across the water. This, then, is where it all began. I touch the water, and closing my eyes, see it all again.

I can see the wide decks of the powerful *Caribee* and her thick teak caprail. I can feel the swift *Ramona* tremble beneath my feet as she runs off the wind. The curve of my lovely *Dubloon*'s stem is as firmly etched in my mind today as it was all those years ago. The *Janeen*'s lofty spars drift across a trade wind sky and I can smell the tarred marlin and linseed oil of the *Windbloweth* and *Nellie J. King*. They are all with me still. I can hear the voices of the men who sailed with me through the years, and the sounds of the wind in the sails and

THE LOGBOOK WAS FULL NOW, AND WE DROPPED ANCHOR FOR THE LAST TIME.

the creaking of block and tackle. I have had it all in fair measure; the good, the bad, the joy, and the sorrow.

And through it all, Terry has stood by me. She has been my pillar of support, my lover, and my confidant. Oh, what I have learned over the years. I am certainly wiser now than at the beginning and perhaps I understand the mystery of life a little better. But who can understand it all? The little flame inside that kept me alive in the lifeboat still burns brightly within, and when I go I will take it with me; it will never go out.

My children have grown and made their way. They have brought me much joy, my sons and daughters, and I am truly blessed. My sons have walked in my footsteps and followed the ocean. Who can ask for more? Lou has sailed the sea as master of sailing vessels and Peter has gone on to build great wooden windships, as it was done in my time. Janeen has found her satisfaction in the written word, while Brian is a shrimp farmer in Honduras. And my little Michelle? She has found her life in Ecuador, where she raises her family and paints wonderful canvases. I know that a little of Terry and me lives within each of our children. They have shown courage and a yearning for adventure. That is my legacy to them.

And so I return to the islands for the last time, to my last ship. She sails no more. The old *High Barbaree* is but a home to me now. I have chosen to live the last of my days on the water and not the land. How could it be otherwise? The old steel ketch is as tired as I am, and I will let her rest in the bay of these warm islands, for she has served me well and I require no more of her.

I sit on the stern and look out towards the west as the sun sets. What has it all meant? What lies beyond? Perhaps at last I have found an answer to the quest that has driven me all my life, but it is mine and mine alone.

And so, I end my story with this simple thought: There resides in everyone the spirit of adventure, that small flame that inspires life's quest. All that is required is the kindling and then it will burn brightly. The first sips of freedom's heady brew are intoxicating and will pull you ever onwards, as it has me. Drink freely of it and you will not be disappointed. May fair winds fill your sails and the lee shore never find you.

The captain died peacefully on November 20, 1996 in Yarmouth, Nova Scotia. I was on passage in mid-Atlantic at the time. I am sure that is where he would have wanted me to be.

Capt. Robert Louis Boudreau
Chester, Nova Scotia, 1998